MW00637961

THE STEPPER

GOD'S RELENTLESS PURSUIT

JERRAD HARDIN

Copyright © 2019 by Jerrad Hardin

All rights reserved. Printed in the United States of America. No part of this book may be used or reproduced in any manner whatsoever without written permission except in the case of brief quotations embodied in critical articles or reviews.

For Questions About Appearances and Speaking Engagements, please contact us here: **Jerrad@444story.com**

FOR GRANDPA

"Smart & Good Lookin', Too."

1931 -2016

The Stepper

Table of Contents

CHAPTER ONE

The Light Switch

John 11:25 *"I am the resurrection and the life. The one who believes in me will live, even though they die."*

"MAYBE IT'S LIKE TURNING OFF A LIGHT."

When I froze, he was left to his own question.

"What do you think happens when we die?" His question bounced around like a ping-pong ball inside my head. A desperate face highlighted by cloudy blue eyes begged for an answer. Inquisitive eyes searching for a warm truth, pleading for a comforting response. Instead, I weakly shook my head.

More than anything I wanted to place his mind at ease — unburden his heart. But the sincerity of the moment required honesty. And, honestly, I had little to no faith. Reflectively, at that moment, I failed him. I failed myself. But, most importantly, I failed God.

There are numerous scriptures from the Bible detailing what happens upon death for the saved and the unsaved. It's clear, for the saved, you'll be in the presence of God. For the unsaved, you'll experience unimaginable suffering through eternal damnation.

My inability to communicate this simple, truthful message to him haunts me to this day. Had I reaffirmed his faith, comforted him with the *Word*, perhaps he would have been unburdened with the idea of death. Regretfully, I lacked the ability, wisdom, and faith to do so.

As we sat there, the sun shone brightly overhead, streaking through the gaps left barren by the trees meant to shade the patio. The breeze gently blew cool through the same set of trees, rattling leaves until they fell one by one to the ground below. Under any other circumstances, it would have been a nearly perfect day.

We were positioned next to one another in opposite ways. His big hands folded as if in prayer, leaning forward with his elbows resting upon his knees. He stared blankly into the distance. It's difficult to say if he was deep in thought or trying his best to avoid it. In contrast, I leaned back in my chair searching for something intelligent to say. It was an uncomfortably quiet moment.

After a short while, he broke the silence using a softer tone. "They say I have cancer, but I don't really believe it." The latter part seemed to trail off as if someone had steadily turned a radio dial backward.

I painfully realized this was no longer a casual conversation. It was obvious his thoughts were focused on the evil seed that had burrowed itself deep in the lower lobe of his right lung.

"What do you think happens when we die?" The thought raced in circles around my brain. Paralyzed. Voiceless. Frozen.

While not asked with urgency, his question was soaked in it. There was no doubt that this was a fact-finding mission. A search for the truth. It required a comforting response. He was seeking my opinion. He valued what I might share. The moment demanded more of me. Yet, I failed.

He continued. "I'm not taking any treatment. It won't make one bit of difference one way or the other." Again, his voice faded.

I hid my tear-filled eyes, looked away and focused on a falling leaf as it floated lower, slowly losing its battle with gravity.

The scene rich with symbolism.

My emotions saturated with guilt, anger, fear. I should've been there more often for him. I hated cancer and what it was going to do to him. I feared for his well-being and questioned my ability to handle his impending decline.

For a moment I thought about God. Did He exist? Would He be there for this man? For our family? If God is there, why is this wretched disease here?

Derailing my train of thoughts, he reasoned, "We all die… That's a guarantee." His voice now confident and bold. His strength and resolve once again on full display.

In response, I looked his way but avoided his eyes.

He unfolded his hands and straightened. "I just wish it wasn't that way."

I stood with the start of a smile and embraced him. Taking note of how he felt. Still strong. He felt like home to me. His strength made me feel small. Here stood the bravest person in my world. He was so much of my world, and I loved him like I had never loved anyone else.

I want to go back to that moment. I wish to relive the entire scene. If it could all be done again, the conversation would be much different. More comforting – more reassuring – more about the promise of God.

"Maybe it's like turning off a light."

"No, Grandpa, death is when the light turns on.

CHAPTER TWO

The Stepper

Proverbs 13:22 *"A good person leaves an inheritance for his children's children."*

"IT'S NOT MUCH FOR A STEPPER."

His voice echoed with a deep quality to it. And if he ever used it in a way to get your attention, his booming voice could easily intimidate.

"You're a *Stepper*, aren't ya?"

Never completely sure, "Yes, Grandpa."

"Well, if you're a *Stepper*, this ain't nothing to worry about," he encouraged.

Without catching his breath, he continued, "*Steppers* step, and this isn't anything to be getting down on your dobber about."

For as long as I can remember, this was the question and reasoning he provided to me, anytime I faced a challenge. Whether I was being bullied at school, striking out in baseball, or failing in a relationship, I was constantly reminded that I was to be a *Stepper*.

Surely, he adopted this approach to the challenges he faced in his own life. Born dirt-floor-poor in a four-walled house during the *Great Depression*, there's little doubt had he not been a Stepper, he would have succumbed to the circumstances of his time.

A product of his unique life experiences, Grandpa was a master story-teller. The likes of which could have rivaled *Dickens* or *Twain*. Effortlessly, he could draw upon memories and paint a picture with colors you never knew existed. He spoke of characters and settings in such detail, you would find yourself sitting next to them and living in their moment.

He mixed stories from his past along with his brilliant imagination and never missed an opportunity to share with a willing audience. Whether there was an audience of one or a room full of people, during a family get-together, when he spoke, everyone listened. They laughed, cried, and left feeling inspired. His brilliant mind and rich voice could yield any emotion he sought – for him it was as practiced as turning a crank to lift a bucket of water from a home-made well.

When his eyes started to squint, it usually previewed what might be coming. From the first word out of his mouth, a deeper quality replaced his typically softer tone.

Grandpa didn't just tell stories, but transported listeners to the scene by transforming himself into the characters he used.

He usually favored comedy, and he was remarkably good at delivering a punchline but equally helpless concealing its arrival. Often, he started laughing before ever finishing a story. The very act seemingly dared you not to laugh along.

While, other times, he might evoke a touching narrative about his life.

When he told me about spending full summer days picking cotton in July, at five-years-old, my fingers seemed to bleed as his once did. Wading the creek behind his childhood home, I felt the coolness of the water waist-deep. As a teenager, he cut timber with a hand-saw in the bottom-country, and my body ached from the back-breaking work. When he went to the Navy, I saw the ocean for the first time. And when he met the love of his life, I knew what real love looked like.

Norman Earl Hardin, my Grandpa – a master story-teller – a *Stepper.*

CHAPTER THREE

The Runner

Matthew 18:12 *"What do you think? If any man has a hundred sheep, and one of them has gone astray, does he not leave the ninety-nine on the mountains and go and search for the one that is straying?"*

"YOU DON'T EXIST!" When I boldly confessed those three words aimed at the darkness, fists clenched, my soul could not have been any farther from God.

Prior to my teenage years, I spent a lot of time in church, sitting through Sunday School, and mumbling along with the choir. Attending church was a prerequisite for staying overnight with my cousins on the weekend. My aunt would have it no other way. I so loved being anywhere other than home and particularly loved spending time with my cousins, the trade-off was one I had to accept.

I never really wanted to go to church. Sleeping-in or going fishing sounded much better, but, again, my aunt was uncompromising.

She had to be relentless as the weekly fight getting us out of bed to out the door was real. Three boys, similar in age, a small trailer home with one shower. The good Lord had blessed my Aunt Jan with a strong voice and stronger resolve. In another life, my aunt could have convinced any fresh-faced platoon to perform endless push-ups in the rain, march in mud for hours under a half-moon, or whatever it is drill sergeants so purposefully encourage undisciplined teenagers to do. It could not have been easy, but somehow, she managed to keep us following orders.

Every Sunday we made our way to the squatty church. A few miles away, it sat near the highway, adorned with orange brick, sitting like an island in a sea of white gravel. The exterior seemed to glow when splashed with sunlight. Inside, glossy oak pews with flat red cushions were split by a narrow-carpeted path leading from the front door directly to the altar. This is where the animated Pastor Woods preached before a white crucifix floating above a tank, highlighted with floodlights, used to wash away sins. His sermons were drenched in passion. Intensity lived upon his face. Sweat ran scared from his brow. His thick arms waved, pleaded, gestured in perfect pace with the pattern of his speech. His captivating voice rattled the stain-glass windows lining the east and west walls of the sanctuary – every Sunday morning, Sunday night and Wednesday evening. And if you were staying overnight with Aunt Jan, you'd bear witness to all three.

Seemingly, Pastor Woods could shout the devil out of your soul while at the same time walk Christ into your heart. I certainly admired him, but he scared the life out of me.

I often felt scared at church. For me, church wasn't a place of love, but one of fear. I was terrified to do the wrong thing, say something incorrect, or act in ways that might encourage Pastor Woods to shout the devil out of me. I followed along without asking questions, doing my best to be obedient. When instructed, I stood, bowed my head, and prayed.

Just before my teenage years, my father accepted a job near Omaha, Nebraska. This meant, my mother, younger brother, and I would be moving. No more Saturday nights with my cousins. No more Sundays with Pastor Woods. No more running away to my grandparents. No more running from a home life I didn't want or understand.

Running. I have done a lot of running. I've been running from many things my entire life. Had I ever taken the time to glimpse over my shoulder, I would have noticed God was running after me.

CHAPTER FOUR

Trucks

James 1:12 *"Blessed is the one who perseveres under trial because, having stood the test, that person will receive the crown of life that the Lord has promised to those who love him."*

"HOW MANY TRUCKS DO YOU SUSPECT GO UP AND DOWN THAT ROAD EACH DAY?"

He liked asking questions like this.

I replied in a sing-song way. "I have no idea."

"There sure is a bunch," his delivery much like mine.

More seriously, he concluded.

"I bet you can't throw a rock across that road without hitting a big truck."

Politely, I agreed.

Traffic was certainly heavy, but from where I sat, the front porch of my grandparents' home in a small town in Arkansas, didn't exactly match my experience with the Kennedy Freeway in Omaha. "Just makes you wonder where everybody's going," He mused.

"Maybe they're going to work or picking up their kids?" I offered.

He turned in his seat and lightly placed his hand on my arm.

"No, I mean, where do you think they're going?" He emphasized the last word as his eyes narrowed and his chin lowered, before adding more emphatically, "In life."

If I were to try, I'd never be able to count the number of conversations we had shared on that front porch with our feet stretched to the railing in front of us, the cigarette between his fingers, a steaming cup of coffee cradled in his hands, hashing out a wide range of topics from politics to why the fish stopped biting. Rarely, did our conversations get philosophical, but this time it had taken that turn.

I hedged. "I guess that's hard to say."

He removed his hand from my arm and assumed his original position. His eyes now strained through horizontal slits. His mouth opened and then closed like a false start before he found the words.

"I just wonder," his voice trembled, then stopped.

I turned in my chair to look at him while gently placing my hand on his forearm.

"What are you thinking about, Grandpa?"

Without looking at me, he held his cigarette in front of him like a pencil between his fingers. The familiar smell of burning tobacco lingered from its ashen-end. His eyes seemed to curse what was left of it as he examined the stubby cylinder with its addictive-toxins casually rolling from the edges of the burning white paper meant to hold it together.

"I've smoked these things nearly all my life." It was a proclamation profoundly stated like the opening line of an Inaugural Address.

The statement stood alone for a few moments before he confessed, "I guess, I've never really believed they could give you cancer." His voice began to stretch. "All my life, people smoked these dadgum things. Never getting sick. Growing old. Some of them outliving their own kids. It's just hard to believe…"

I listened as he went on.

"And the heckuva it is, the tobacco companies sell it to you in their ads like you're really somebody special when you're holding one of these." With agitation, he showed it to me for emphasis before angrily dismissing the repulsive thing by flicking it from his tar-stained fingers onto the yard, beyond the porch.

From my view of his profile, his chiseled jaw grew increasingly tense as he squeezed his eyes shut, hiding his pain.

I waited.

"Grandma has been on my butt for as long as I can remember. At first, she didn't want me smoking in the house. Then, in the truck. Before long, not at all. She never did like me smoking…Truth is, I don't know if I liked it either." He stiffened, and lamented, "I should've listened to her."

It had to be a painful admission. I respected his genuine honesty, and he likely wanted me to agree with him, but now was not the time to pile on.

"You couldn't have known," I reasoned.

He countered quickly, "Grandma knew."

I shot back with a smile, "If we all knew what Grandma knew, the world wouldn't have any need for questions."

He looked at me with a short grin.

Then, he relaxed and leveled, "Jerrad, I've lived a good life. A real good life. When I was a kid, I couldn't even have dreamed my life would be so good. All the blessings I've had couldn't be stacked up and counted if you had a team of workers on it full-time. The things I've gotten to do, the things I've accomplished, my family..." The latter seemed to punch him in the gut. "Only complaint is, seems like I blinked, and it was over..." The admission was like a surprising haymaker delivered squarely on his chin.

"I'm sorry." I meant it.

"Don't be," he replied softly.

After a deep breath, he laid bare his soul, "Before the doctors said I had cancer, I always felt like I'd just been sitting around waiting to die." His voice cracked. "It's just…really I wasn't."

I watched the remains of the smoldering cigarette die in the grass before us. I hated it. I despised what it had done to this man. Whatever enjoyment he had gained from it felt small compared to the pain it heaped upon our family.

My attention turned back to him. "Grandpa, are you scared?"

He considered the question before answering.

"…No, no, I'm not really scared. There's nothing to be afraid of… I guess." His tone suggested otherwise. "I'm just not ready to go."

This, I believed.

His vulnerability made my stomach flip.

"Is there anything I can do to help?"

I was pleading as much as posing a question.

He rubbed his head with a hand big enough to cover his entire face. Then, without ever opening his eyes, he muttered, "Nothing I can think of."

His response left me feeling hopeless. The contents of my stomach churned into my throat leaving a sour taste in my mouth.

I assumed my position, facing forward, feet on the porch railing. I sat hoping for everything, while staring at the wide nothing, looming in the space between me and the highway.

For the next few minutes, we sat alone in our own somber thoughts. In the background, a symphony of birds chirped back and forth amongst the tall trees lining the driveway. Briefly, it caught my attention and my mind drifted for the next few moments as I scanned the trees while considering the number of birds who may have listened to our conversation.

Before I found the answer, Grandpa stood up and said, "At least a hundred or more." A grin stretched across his face as he looked down at me.

With a puzzled expression, I studied him.

"I'm figuring, that's how many trucks go up and down that road every day." He laughed in a way that made you wonder if he might ever catch his breath. His eyes squeezed shut like a vise, shoulders hunched forward, hands spread wide, body bouncing like a pogo stick in slow motion, all the while his generous mouth hollowed by happiness with hardly a sound escaping. Grandpa's signature laugh.

Shaking my head, I found it impossible not to laugh along with him. I moved my feet from the railing, just so he could pass.

Alone, I briefly wondered how many conversations on that porch I might have left with him.

I had no way to know, so I resigned myself to listening to the sounds made by chatty birds while passively counting trucks zooming up and down the road.

CHAPTER FIVE

Angel

Proverbs 31:26 *"She opens her mouth with wisdom, and the teaching of kindness is on her tongue?"*

"Hello, Angel!" It was a name I was surely unworthy of holding, but to my Grandma Hazel, I would be addressed in no other way.

"Grandma, where's Grandpa?" I had barely made it through the door. It was rushed and unintentionally rude. But at ten-years-old, I had not fully developed politeness or patience.

"Well, let's see, last I heard he was going to check some cows over at the Scroggins' place." Her answer was given in the most harmonious way. She wiped her hands together with a dish towel and opened her arms for a hug. I didn't hesitate to fall into her warm embrace.

"Why didn't he wait for me?" I complained. "I wanted to go."

"I'm sorry Angel," always sincere. "Why don't we go on in here and have a bite to eat so we can talk about it – I made some cookies," she added.

Grandma was an expert in the kitchen and a made the best chocolate chip cookies you could ever imagine. The smell alone triggered some unexplainable suppressed craving that seemed to leap to life upon the first whiff. Before ever taking a bite, you imagined the explosion of sweetness dissolving in your mouth. As a result, when presented with a plate full of the tasty treats, you found yourself acting like Fred Flintstone attacking a Brontosaurus Burger after work.

We sat across from one another at the kitchen table, a plate loaded with cookies between us. "What else can I get you?" She had already poured a tall glass of milk and placed it next to me.

"Nothing, Grandma, thank you." Cookies seemed to encourage politeness.

Curiously she asked, "What's happenin' at your house this mornin'?" If you don't know, G's are optional in the South.

Before I could respond, I had to wash down what was left of the cookie residue in my mouth. I grabbed the cold glass of milk, lowered its ceiling by half, then explained, "Well, Momma and Daddy were playing cards all night with some people, poker I figured, so they were still asleep when I left, and Shelby, he didn't want to come with me." Shelby, my sole sibling, a brother, younger by four years.

Grandma simply smiled and held her gaze directly on me. "Well, I'm tickled you come to see me." This was evident.

The house I lived in sat directly across the highway from the brick house where my grandparents lived. There are few memories worth holding onto from that drafty old white house, which I never called home. My home was and will always be the dark brick house built across the way, atop a hill at the end of a long curvy white-rock driveway set in the middle of the woods. A place where memories made were worth keeping.

More time was spent darting across the busy highway than was ever spent in that cold bedroom located in the back of the old white house. Naturally then, much of my childhood was spent with either Grandma, Grandpa or both - eating anything she wanted to feed me and tagging along anywhere he wanted to go.

"Grandma, I did come to see you," I fibbed and paused to lick the melted chocolate from my fingers, "but, I was also looking for Grandpa."

She found humor in my response before offering, "Maybe he'll be back shortly."

I finished off the glass of milk.

"Have I told you how much I love you, lately?" The tip of her tongue peeked ever-so-slightly through her pretty teeth as she smiled with adoration.

After shaving the milk mustache with the back of my hand, "Grandma, you always say that." I pretended not to want to hear it.

"Angel, did you know God made you special? And He's got so many great things planned for you." She reached across the table and squeezed my hand. "God will always be there for you – just read your

Bible, talk to Him, tell Him your needs, never lie, follow His *Word*, and never stop believing that He loves you, as much or more than I do."

I smiled warmly and squeezed her hand. "Grandma, nobody could love me more than you – not even God." It was meant to be a serious response.

She tried to cover her laugh with her hand but bits of it spilled around the edges.

Composed, she replied, "You are such a blessing, Angel, and we are so, so proud of you and your brother – me and Grandpa just couldn't possibly love you more than we do."

It wasn't an exaggeration. My grandparents were champions of love. Without conditions, they knew how to love, how to show that love, and how to make one feel loved. This was unquestionable. Sadly, for many years to come, I would find myself questioning what she attempted teaching me about God.

She stretched her neck to peer beyond from where she sat at the table, through the living room, to a large set of picture windows providing a view to the front yard.

"I think I see Grandpa coming up the drive." Her eyes swung back to me, wide with excitement, she said, "Maybe you and Grandpa can go to the pond and catch us a mess of fish to eat for supper!"

Seemingly she had read my mind. Grinning from ear to ear, I reached for another cookie.

CHAPTER SIX

Pretty Eyes

Hebrews 11:1 *"Now faith is the assurance of things hoped for, the conviction of things not seen."*

"OH, OH, OH!" Santa-like but the letters in reverse.

"What pretty little eyes he's got!"

All of this followed by his signature laugh as he masterfully twisted the sharp barb from the mouth of the latest *whopper* he managed to pull from the water.

I don't know which expression held more shock, mine or that of the trophy-like bass he proudly bragged about – eyes twice their normal size, mouths wide open, and both shaking our heads.

"You've got to be kidding me," I finally managed to say. I was complaining more than complimenting him as he tossed the fish back

"What's the matter?" It came out in gusts as he laughed so hard, I thought he might follow the fish back into the water.

"We should'a took a picture." By his reaction, this seemed much funnier to him than it was to me. Through a burst of laughter, he tried, "I'd have even let you hold him for a..." Certainly, he was suggesting

I could have taken a picture with it, but he was taken away, overcome with pure joy, before the offer could fully be made.

I headed for his truck parked alongside the pond bank, tossed my fishing pole and tackle into the back. I leaned against its door, one foot on the ground another propped behind me, and wondered just how he did it.

He turned to look at me, still bouncing with laughter his posture surrendering to the gut-busting humor he found himself enjoying so much, an impossibly big finger pointing in my direction from one hand as he supported himself with the other atop a bent knee. I don't know how he remained standing; it defied the laws of physics.

"Hey, you're not mad are ya?" He barely got it out, rushing to finish, just before he doubled over in laughter again, bellowing in such a way that made tears form at the corners of his eyes.

My grandpa loved fishing almost as much as he loved bragging about his good fortune pulling a lunker from the water. Here I was, forty years old, witnessing my own personal version of the movie *Groundhog Day*. Every time we went fishing, for as long as I could remember, Grandpa caught fish, even when nobody else did. And, he loved to let you know about it in his own unique ways.

Somehow, he pulled himself upright and strolled to the truck. Each of his steps, a happy one.

"How come you're quittin'? His watery eyes twinkling above a cartoon grin.

"I'm done." Flatly.

This sparked his signature laugh again, only to be interrupted by another idea. Without skipping a beat, he broke out a tired-old tune he liked to sing when he really wanted to get your goat.

"You got to know when to hold 'em, know when to fold em', know when to set the hook, no when to let em' run."

The old man sounded like a carbon copy of Hank Williams - not the *Country Boy Can Survive* Hank Williams, but the original crooner, the *Hey Good Lookin'* Hank Williams.

He never missed the chance to-rub-it-in-when-you-lose-the-big-fish.

Though, the song never made it any farther than the opening lines before he'd succumb to his own laughter. I'm unsure if there was any more to his version, there certainly didn't need to be, that was as much as anyone ever needed to hear.

The August heat reflected off the side of the red Ford, as I leaned against it waiting for the final act of Grandpa's comedy routine to finish up. It had been particularly hot that summer, his last summer.

Going fishing seemed like a good idea. He needed to get out of the house, and I yearned for as many final memories as I could steal before the poison growing inside him took him away from us forever.

As he rested his body against the truck, next to me, I moved my arm behind him and gently pulled him closer with a half-hug. "So, are you ever going to tell me your secret before you kick the bucket?" I was only partially joking.

He reached over and gave me a full hug, a big smile on his face. He took a long step away, took a half-turn and scanned the sky above us. as I waited.

Looking at him, I couldn't help but see how the frame of this bigger-than-life character had shrunk. His favorite snap-button western shirt hung loosely from his formerly broad shoulders. His faded brown leather belt boasted two freshly-handmade notches. His plain blue jeans continued to slide down from his hips, making his long legs seem shorter.

It was amazing how quickly his body had diminished. Just a few months before he was still standing a head above most people and most of the ropy muscle from his physical peak remained. Now, he was shrinking, small. Helpless. Hopeless.

"You gotta believe," he said it without looking at me, eyes still surveying the clouds.

"What do you believe in, Grandpa?"

He glanced over.

"I reckon most days I believe in just about anything and I wanna believe in everything."

"That's a good way of looking at things," I responded.

He slowly moved his hands into his pockets, covering mostly just his fingers. He squeezed his shoulders as if he might be cold. "Just take that fish I caught." He nodded in the direction of the pond. "I was certain, without any doubt whatsoever, I was going to catch him before I ever tried."

I chuckled and argued, "No, you didn't."

His piercing eyes turned back to me, and he quickly countered, "Of course I did, and If I hadn't, I wouldn't have caught him."

I tried to reason, "There's just no possible way you knew that you were going to catch a fish, that fish, or any other fish before you ever even cast your bait into the water – just isn't possible."

He grinned with a hint of agitation. "You're not a believer."

"I'm a realist." I said it defensively but tried to offset it with a kind smirk.

"Well, if you can't believe what I just told you, you may as well not believe in anything at'all." He was clearly trying to get this point across.

I lowered my head, kicking at the dry grass, finally asking, "Is that your secret to catching fish? Just believe you can?"

In a serious tone, the one he took when something was of great importance to him, he spoke deliberately. "That's the secret to e-very-thing." He seemed to spell out the last word as he stated it with emphasis.

The powerful meaning and delivery of the statement brought pause to the moment.

My foot stopped kicking at the grass. We stood facing one another, he had shortened the distance between us, his hands still wedged into shallow pockets. We stared at one another, his face suggesting that he just shared the most important lesson of my life. Mine, thankful for his gift.

He brought his hands from his pockets, held his arms out wide, fingers spread, and uttered but a single word, "Faith."

CHAPTER SEVEN

The Good Life

---

1 Peter 5:10 *"And after you have suffered a little while, the God of all grace, who has called you to his eternal glory in Christ, will himself restore, confirm, strengthen, and establish you."*

... the good life – The state motto set prominently in white letters on a green road sign– NEBRASKA. Home of Arbor Day, Chimney Rock, and rabid football fans who oddly adorned exaggerated corncobs for hats on gamedays.

Nebraska, our new adventure.

Nebraska, where eighth-grade awaited.

Nebraska, the good life – though, at the time, you could have fooled me.

"There it is," mom gestured out the window, motioning to it with a smoldering cigarette squeezed between her fingers as she held firm to the steering wheel.

Groggy from the long drive, my brother and I stood from the backseat supporting ourselves against the headrests in front of us. My suspicious gaze detected nothing but fields and fields full of corn, casting a sea of dark green shadows across a flattened landscape. From my view, an infinite amount of corn stalks set between perfectly drawn rows, lying motionless beneath an impossibly large, cloudless sky.

It looked nothing like I had imagined. The analogous scenery was a vast contrast to the towering pines and shady oaks of the Ozark foothills.

This faraway land, where my dad's work in road construction was bringing our family, appeared as void of people as it was of trees.

"Look at all the corn, boys!" She dared a glance over her shoulder. "This is going to be good for you boys – good for all of us." That latter said in a whisper of hope.

My father awaited our arrival in a small apartment above an even smaller fitness center in the downtown area of an unremarkable town set somewhere between Lincoln and Omaha. When we arrived, my first impression of our new dwelling was that it felt cool and smelled of fresh paint and new carpet. These were foreign smells I enjoyed.

The apartment lay mostly bare. There were no furnishings but for a small wooden table accompanied by two mismatched chairs pushed near a wall in a tiny area meant to be a kitchen. In the living space, a square television sat alone on the floor tailed by a long black cord with its end stuck into the wall. There were two bedrooms and a shared bathroom with a single sink and a small shower & tub combo. A large mattress was centered on the floor of my parents' room. In a room directly across a narrow hall, my brother and I were assigned smaller individual mattresses in a parallel arrangement on the floor.

After the short tour of our new living situation, we stood around in the living area like strangers, at a loss for ideas and waiting for direction. It wasn't the first time we were trying-on what being a family was like, and this time didn't seem destined to be any more successful than our previous attempts. After some awkwardness, we decided on a bite to eat, after which we stretched at various angles around the television, before eventually giving up, retiring to our new sleeping arrangements.

The general excitement of moving was quickly replaced with a deep longing for those in another place. I missed my cousins, friends, and grandparents. Reconnecting with a phone call meant a long-distance fee, and it was more than I could muster for the payphone on the corner.

But after a few weeks, I found myself hurting for my grandparents. Unable to wait any longer, or muster up the nerve to ask for money, I dialed them collect.

After a question, an agreement was made between the operator and my grandpa, the line connected. With the receiver against my ear and a smile on my face, the humming of the line seemed to mute as an audible click was followed by my grandpa's distinctive voice.

"Hey!" he said, and you could hear the joy in his greeting.

"Grandpa!"

He didn't waste any time, "Are you a *corn-hoer*, yet?" A deep laugh followed.

"Grandpa!" This time it came out elongated with a dash of whine.

"Ahhh-Shah, I figured you'd found you a pretty corn-fed girl, and got you a job hoeing corn by now."

I ignored his silliness. "Is Grandma home?"

He found humor in the deflection before surrendering to a softer tone. "No, Grandma had to run to the store. She'll hate to hear that she missed you."

"That's, okay." My general sadness was hard to hide.

"What's the matter?" His concern was authentic.

I complained, "I don't like it here." It was a statement of truth. "I want to come home – I miss you."

"Well, now, you need to give it a chance." The fact was he didn't like us being gone any more than I liked it, and his response was half-hearted at best.

"Grandpa, momma and dad are always gone, working. Me and Shelby have been by ourselves almost every day. We ain't got nobody here to do anything with. We don't know anybody. Kids at school aren't real nice. I just want to come home."

He listened to my list of grievances without interrupting.

When he replied, it was firm. "I know you don't want to hear it, but your mom and dad are doing what they think is best. You'll find in life there's going to be a whole bunch of things you don't like, don't understand, don't want."

He stopped for a moment as if lining up his next string of thoughts with absolute precision.

Then with more conviction, he stated, "Being uncomfortable is going to make you a better, stronger person. Learning to trust and believe that things will be alright, even when it don't seem that way, will get you on past it. And, no matter how bad you think your situation is – it could always be worse."

Without question, he knew this from his childhood experience.

I wanted to say, "BUT, Grandpa", but I didn't dare. I only managed a dispassionate, "Okay."

"I love you," he meant it. "I'll tell Grandma you called. You take care of Shelby and do your best. It'll all get better."

Again, "Okay."

"You're a *Stepper* aren't ya?"

I could tell he was smiling now. "I love you, Grandpa."

As the days faded into weeks, my free time was spent dribbling a basketball to and from a local playground just a few blocks from our lonesome apartment. My parents squeezed every ray of sunshine out of their workday, leaving my brother and me to entertain and care for ourselves.

While my time was spent alone pounding my feelings into an orange rubber-coated ball worn slick with use, I'm unsure and saddened to think about how Shelby must have spent his time in solitude.

As it turned out, all that time my parents spent at work and all of which they sacrificed in hopes of creating a *good life* for our family, ultimately, couldn't outweigh the problems that existed in their marriage.

Before the falling leaves turned to blustery stinging pellets of snow, we were on the move again. This time west, to a small community set along an east-west interstate highway and the Platte River. We were to meet my father there, but unbeknownst to me, other plans had been made. However, as Grandpa had instructed, I did my best to trust and believe that everything would be alright.

Once we arrived in our new surroundings, we settled into a trailer park perched on the edge of town. It was nothing more than three vertical rows of stubby well-faded rectangles set in symmetry on a square plot of dirt that looked to be abandoned by the city. For the remainder of the school year, three of us occupied the tired space, while the fourth member of our disjointed family never showed.

After a few weeks of not seeing my father, I remember waking one night to find that he was unexpectedly in my room. On my bed, behind me with his arms wrapped around me, his chest pressed against my back, my head tucked beneath his chin. His embrace was comforting, and without acknowledging his presence, I fell back asleep. It was the warmest, most affectionate moment involving my dad from my entire childhood. When I woke, he was gone.

That evening my mother sat across from us and explained that our dad had visited late the night before. She struggled with her emotions as she searched for the right words. As if thrown a lifeline, the shrill ring of the telephone saved her from further explanation. She answered the call and after a few terse words she pushed the phone receiver to me and nodded for me to take it.

The awkwardly heavy receiver pressed flat against the side of my head. I may have known what was coming, but I expected the message to be difficult for him to deliver.

He found the words in the first line. "Son, I'm not coming back."

Hearing it stung sharply. There were more prepared words spoken, but they seemed to be drowned out by the opening remark. As he finished, I was able to focus enough to hear him say, "You'll need to be the man of the house, take care of your momma and Shelby." It was a misplaced appointment of responsibility that didn't match my age or level of preparedness.

After setting the receiver down, I squeezed beads of tears from my eyes and quickly sought refuge behind the thin door of my room.

Lying on my bed, I wondered how God could be so cruel. Abandoning faith, I rolled onto my side, wrapped my arms around my pillow and cried myself to sleep, feeling certain that it no longer made sense to believe in anything. My world had been shattered by a single sentence from my father's mouth. How could I possibly trust that it would all be okay?

CHAPTER EIGHT

Flipped

Deuteronomy 20:4 ""For the LORD your God is He who goes with you, to fight for you against your enemies, to save you."

"IT WAS A DEER!"

It wasn't. But rather an excuse born from an urgent need.

He faced me gripping my shoulders as I struggled to stand. He repeated it while trying to desperately explain the truth away.

He insisted, "It was a deer and it ran out in front of us." Then unsure, "Are you hearing me?"

Before nodding, I inspected the spring of blood above my brow. There was a steady stream running past my nose to the edge of my face.

"You okay?" His worry, shifting to me.

I managed to nod.

As I looked beyond him, shock invaded my senses. My brain had been shaken ruthlessly, without any regards for the contents.

Suddenly, I swayed, uneasy on my feet, like the ground started spinning away from where I wanted to go.

"We have to get you to the hospital, sit down." His worry turned to fear as he hopelessly surveyed our options. Unfortunately, we were surrounded by helpless ears of corn.

Cory, my best friend who I had nearly just killed, helped to ease me off my feet, slumping me along the edge of the gravel road.

My mother's sweet Mustang lay belly-up, stretched across a deep irrigation ditch. White puffs rolled out from the front-end appearing like smoke in one of the old Westerns I had watched a few years earlier with Grandpa. Shreds of a back tire hung loosely from a chrome wheel reflecting the afternoon sun. Glass was sprinkled all about either from the nose smashing the opposite side of the embankment or the flip that left us with our tires in the air. The roof collapsed leaving jagged exits on each side. But I was alive. Surely, I was alive given the rapid pulse felt in my temples and the hurried chase for my next breath.

I heard the hiss of a motor more accustomed to humming, clouded in a stench of steaming anti-freeze mixed with unsettled dust, and singed oil, leaving a dirty smell in the air. The odor mixed with the throbbing in my head nearly made me lose my lunch.

Cory remained unfazed in his denial for what had really happened.

"We swerved to miss a deer. That's what we tell them," he said, less panicked now, almost convincing himself it was the truth.

I dropped my head, folded my arms across a pair of drawn-up knees, and watched the blood drip from my nose forming a small pool of blood between my feet.

Merely weeks after getting my license, I felt an immediate realization that I was lucky to be alive.

My mother's car, the only thing we owned, now flopped upside down in a ditch after spinning on a gravel road, miles from town, during an unseasonably warm, perfect fall day.

When the car began to swerve, I had over-corrected, panicked, and then missed the brakes by slamming my foot onto the gas pedal.

The bright red Mustang Mach-1 wasted no time leaping forward as it had been engineered to do. At a complete loss for control, I found myself in a state of paralysis, with every muscle clenched tight against my bones, a heavy foot cemented atop the accelerator, while my white knuckled hands held fast to the steering wheel.

My life did not flash before my eyes, but a field of corn did, just as the front of my mother's car vacated the road on the left-side and flew across the nearly 15' wide irrigation ditch running parallel to the roadway.

When the car slammed into the dirt embankment, it must have looked like the automobile crash-test dummy ad campaigns of my youth. Those were intended to demonstrate the dire need to wear seatbelts while driving. In this case, my friend and I had not learned *a lot from a dummy*. Without a seatbelt to hold me in place, my forehead slammed against the steering wheel, jolting me into a dream-like state.

The remaining details of this nightmarish ride play out in in slow-motion in my memory.

There was an instantaneous feeling of zero-gravity, as Cory's screams ripped through with an endless voice above the sounds of shattering glass.

In that moment, I had a terrifying realization that life was over.

In the shortest of flashes, it all seemed to be happening as if I might be alone in a windowless room, reading a book, in peaceful silence. But that moment was quickly displaced by the crude and sudden noise of the glass surrendering to the crushing metal surrounding it.

At last, there was a gruesome thud.

Somehow, we both crawled from the wreckage.

One with a cut to the forehead. The other without a scratch.

Somehow both sat together by the roadside.

When a passerby drove upon the scene, he hustled us into his truck and raced to his farmhouse to call for help. Along the way, he cussed us both and lectured us on how lucky we had been to survive.

My head continued to spin as Cory tried our sad excuse on the passerby. All I could think was how that poor imaginary deer was taking all the blame.

Throughout the late afternoon a stream of visitors stopped by the hospital to check on me.

Then, early in the evening, I had to provide a statement to law enforcement.

"You know you're lucky to be alive." The serious tone of the Trooper standing by my bedside was hard to ignore.

"I know," I agreed.

"So, are you sticking to your story? You swerved to miss a deer." His question sounded like a song, and his statement full of mockery.

"If that's what Cory says." It was evasive at best.

He countered, "Son, there were no deer tracks in the vicinity, but it really doesn't matter one way or the other what caused the accident. The fact that you survived it is what's really important."

The Trooper let his arms fall to his sides and he gripped my bed railing for support. His eyes narrowed with sincerity as he leaned forward. He carefully gathered his thoughts before saying, "This was more than luck."

It was the way he said it that brought my full attention to his expression.

He shook his head first, then grinned. "The one thing none of us on the scene could figure is how you left that road at better than 90 mph by our estimates, neither of you had a seatbelt on, you slammed against the opposite side of the ditch, flipped in the air, and the car somehow, miraculously, landed in a manner that the front end and the back end were supported by each side of the ditch so that the roof didn't completely flatten and crush the two of you."

His eyes locked on mine, and I trembled – his reminder of the hours before rocking me deeply.

"Young man, that's something more than luck. It's something divine. Someone from up above looking out for you." He straightened his frame and released his grip from the bed.

"God was with you today." He said it with such confidence, pursed his lips and gave me a nod, folded his notebook and left me alone to ponder his assessment of my nightmarish afternoon.

The room was dark, it smelled sterile from the overuse of disinfectant, and but for a few nurses talking down the hallway, it was silent.

I stared above my bed to a shadowy white-paneled ceiling and wondered if the Trooper had been correct. Could God have intervened and saved my life? And if so, why? I had not been faithful to Him. I had been running away from Him for years.

I wasn't even sure if He existed outside of my hope for His existence. But if not, how could I explain the improbable survival of the accident I had just experienced. My condition was making it nearly impossible to think clearly, but nonetheless I arrived at a convenient answer.

Closing my eyes, lying motionless on my back, the words spilled out.

"It had to be luck."

CHAPTER NINE

Good Boy

Matthew 16:27 *"For the Son of Man is going to come in his Father's glory with his angels, and then he will reward each person according to what they have done."*

"WHAT DID YOU SAY?" My mother sat straight up from her bed with wide eyes, shocked by my retelling of a vivid dream I had just experienced. The dream had awakened me, it felt so real, and left me with a question that I hoped my mother could answer.

When I eased onto her bed with watery eyes, she had been slow to wake. It was a challenging time for us, and I know she was exhausted. My high school graduation was only a couple of weeks away and she had been working extra shifts at the bar serving up bad habits where her southern charm and a convincing smile left those Nebraska boys reaching deep into their pockets for tips. Even with the extra money, it wasn't enough.

We were accustomed to living on a shoe-string budget, but it worsened after my mother and father divorced. The five-year stretch between his departure and my high school graduation was marked by hard times. Some winters our house stayed ice-cold, the fridge was mostly vacant, and how the water coming from the shower head remained in liquid form is still beyond me. It wasn't as if my mother didn't try, she worked herself to the bone. But she had her own bad habits and the burden of shouldering all the bills became overwhelming. My brother, Shelby, had long-since moved away to live with our father; even then, the costs of raising one child were more than a small-town bartender could afford. Earlier that evening, my mother's mom, who I lovingly knew as Ma, had called to tell us that my grandpa, my mother's stepdad, Joe, had passed.

My mother's biological dad had passed from a heart attack while she was pregnant with me, and my Ma moved on a little too quickly for some in the family by meeting Joe, a Florida real-estate entrepreneur. Ma and Joe wasted no time falling in love and somehow, she convinced him to sell his Florida rental properties and move to Arkansas to marry and live with her. Therefore, I grew up with Joe as my grandpa. I knew nothing of his past, had no preconceived ideas of who he was, and allowed myself to share a strong bond with him. Joe made it a point to frequently tell me that I was his favorite.

During my childhood, I spent lots of time pestering Joe and trying to trip his trigger. Eventually, after exhausting more patience than deserved, he would start firing off words I couldn't understand blended together with his thick Hungarian accent. My laughter always seemed to disarm him, to which he would shake his head and wag his finger at me before saying, "Yoy, Yoy, Yoy, *Bubba*, you gonna get it." I would later find that he called me *Bubba* because his native tongue found it difficult to work in ways to properly say, *Jerrad*.

He was short and round, clean-cut and always neatly dressed. When I visited him a few months before his passing, I was immediately taken aback by his appearance. According to my Ma, my once vibrant Joe now spent most days in a full-sized bed crammed into a quiet, tiny back bedroom.

When I walked in and witnessed him lying on his back with covers pulled to his chin, my lungs were instantly filled with a rush of forced air – in which I held onto and struggled to release. The sight of his pale-yellowed skin, every age spot highlighted against a ghostly background, the frail and weakened state of his once-robust body, and the unique scent of death and decay filling the empty space between us, it all but stole the breath from me.

"Joe?" The word came out softly and as if I was unsure it was really him.

Two dark tiny slits appeared beneath bushy eyebrows. "Bub-ba," the word crawled out in two distinctive parts.

I was afraid to touch him and only let the tips of my fingers rest against his upper arm.

"Joe, how are you feeling?"

"Ohhhh, Bub-ba," he agonized, "I'm not so good."

I let the full surface of my hand rest upon his arm as I grimaced.

"Liver Cancer!" He said it with a notable rise in his voice as if he might be angered to admit it.

"I'm really sorry, Joe." My eyes wet at the edges.

He expelled energy he didn't have by waving his hand dismissively before covering his mouth with the same hand to cover a coughing spell.

"Bubba," he spoke a little more clearly now, "I'm going to die, and I don't have much time left."

"No, don't say that. I need you to hold on for just a few months. I'll be graduating and then I'm coming back to be with you – see you back to health."

His eyes closed, and a thin smile formed. He either liked the thought, or he found humor in my naivety. Whichever, that single image of Joe was burned into my memory, for it was the last time I would see him alive.

On the evening of that dreaded phone call, I listened to my mother as she received the news of his death, she seemed concerned and expressed customary condolences and then handed the phone to me.

"Jerrad," her voice louder than I expected, "this is your Ma." Something I had already ascertained.

"Hi, Ma."

Straightforward, "Joe died tonight in the hospital." She sniffled and stuttered before continuing. "I think you ought to know that before he died all he did was talk about you. It was Bubba this and Bubba that." This seemed to tickle her. "He kept saying Bubba is here and I'd say 'No, he's not', and he'd say 'Yes, he's right over there', pointing to some place over in the corner."

I didn't know what to say, the news of his passing was expected, but learning about it was something altogether different. It was, however, touching to know that I had been on his mind before he passed.

She went on, "Anyway, I thought you ought to know that he couldn't stop thinking about you and talking about you right up until he quit breathing." She emphasized, "he loved you more than anybody."

Grief-stricken and suddenly feeling guilty about not being there for someone who loved me so much, I lost it - unable to respond with anything more than a muffled acknowledgment that came out more like a hiccup.

My mother took the phone and finished the conversation. I fell onto the couch and wept. My mother ran her fingers along my back and spoke comforting words that I was unable to appreciate. At some point, I had cried myself to sleep in the same position where I had fallen onto the couch with grief. Then it happened.

A dream so vivid and so very real it imprinted a memory that still impacts me 25 years later. When I think about the occurrence or retell it, my skin prickles as if it is still happening.

In my sleep, Joe, or some version of Joe appeared to me. Immediately I recognized this mass of energy which hovered above me as my grandpa who had just passed, but he did not possess any characteristics that would make him identifiable. But, despite that, I knew it was him.

Immediately, I called out to him and reached upward in his direction. He was visibly there, but still far beyond my touch.

"Joe!" I shouted to him in amazement.

"Bubba," he responded with a voice I knew at once.

"Listen, I don't have much time, but I have to tell you something." His voice unexpectantly anxious, thick with fear.

I interrupted in the same vein, "Where are you?"

"Listen!" This time he shouted. "Be a good boy – whatever you do in life – BE A GOOD BOY!"

"Where are you?" I pleaded.

"You don't want to be where I am. I'm caught somewhere between heaven and hell and I don't know where I'm going – BE A GOOD BOY!"

"I don't under –" He abruptly interrupted me before I could finish.

"I have to go now, I'm running out of time!"

"Where?" The words sprinted from my mouth.

"I have to go now before it's too late – I have to find Margaret!"

With those words, he was gone, and I was instantly jolted into consciousness.

I found myself sitting up stiffly from where I had collapsed in grief hours before, one arm extended above my head reaching toward emptiness, my body trembled, the hair on my head was wet around the edges from perspiration, and my clothes damp with sweat. I steadied myself and walked from the living room to the rear of the house where my mother slept.

I was never more in need of her warm embrace, her unconditional love, and for an answer, I was sure only she, at this moment, could provide.

"What's wrong, baby?" It came out sluggish.

She barely moved and didn't open her eyes. I moved onto the bed beside her and began describing the dream I had just experienced. It was difficult to know if she was truly listening as she appeared to be sleeping.

"And then he said he had to go – he had to find someone named Margaret before it was too late."

My mother shot up wide-eyed, no longer half-asleep, her eyebrows sharpened in a heavy expression. "What did you say?" It sounded more panicked than inquisitive.

"He said he had to go find Margaret," I repeated.

Her face left no doubt that she was shocked by the words.

"Mom, who is Margaret?"

Her answer was revealed slowly, as if she couldn't believe what she was about to say. "Margaret was Joe's first wife. She had died well before you were born."

"Mom, I didn't even know Joe had a life before us. How could I have known he was married, had a wife, that she died?"

"There's no way you could have."

The immediate realization that what had happened could not have simply been a dream put me flat on my back, my hair on end, every nerve ending tingling, and I found myself confessing aloud, "I'm going to be a good boy."

CHAPTER TEN

Sticks

Matthew 24:36 *"But concerning that day and hour no one knows, not even the angels of heaven, nor the Son, but the Father only."*

"DID I EVER TELL YOU ABOUT..." It was a familiar refrain. Tired but welcome, it was the way he prefaced every joke or story which he could hardly wait to tell. This time, of course, I had heard it before, in fact, many times before. But, as always, I demonstrated a feigned interest in hearing it again. For it wasn't the content, but his delivery I thoroughly enjoyed.

I had recently graduated high school, considered continuing my education and play baseball at a small college in Nebraska, before ultimately getting cold feet and backing out before Freshman Orientation even began. When I called Grandma and Grandpa to share my decision, it was Grandpa who insisted that I wasn't going to be sitting around twiddling my thumbs. Instead, he suggested I move home to Arkansas, live with them, and work on the farm until I figured it out. Without a better option, I agreed.

A few weeks in, I was beginning to find comfort in the routines of farm life. After all, I had spent most of my childhood stacking feed sacks, listening to Grandpa talk about cows while riding shotgun in his truck, and stringing new lines of barbed wire fence around the acres of pasture. However, this was different. No longer was I tagging along for fun, but now I had a schedule with concrete expectations that had to be met daily. I quickly learned that on the farm, there was always something to be done.

On one crisp, cloudless fall afternoon, while virtually all my friends were half-way through completing Freshmen English, I was sitting next to my grandpa on the tailgate of his old Ford. He had finally relented and agreed to a well-earned break. Clearing brush, or bush hogging as we called it, was a big job.

With some much-needed help now in place, Grandpa had purchased an additional stretch of land, connected to his existing property. Then, we were tasked with transforming the land from a briar-infested mess to a blank canvas ready for planting. We needed to quickly clear the land and seed the ground. The extra space would allow Grandpa to purchase yearlings at the sale, fatten them with good pasture grass, alfalfa and powdered corn before shipping them off to a feed-yard somewhere in Texas to maximize their weight gain before they sold at market.

It was an ambitious plan, and the old tractor used to pull the mower had seen better days. Bought second-hand, it was hard to tell if it was painted orange or simply rusting away. Each morning when the contrary machine sputtered, Grandpa would tinker around the engine wondering aloud in disbelief as to why it wasn't working. Meanwhile, I stood next to him and played along, hopelessly wishing he might not be able to get it running so that I could go home and disappear beneath the covers of my bed. Of course, it was a fantasy to believe that Grandpa would ever let me off that easy.

Eventually, his signature combination of colorful language and creative tinkering, he would convince the old tractor to cooperate. Above the roar of the gurgling engine, he grinned and bragged about what a wonderful piece of machinery it was, ignoring that he had spent the first hour of the day cussing the stubborn old thing and manipulating it until it finally relented. Much like I had acted with him as I clamored for a break.

We sat there with the backside of our knees resting on the scarred edge of the tailgate, feet swinging near the ground, leather gloved-hands gripping the same edge. Sweat stung every poke and scratch I had received from wrestling patches of stickers that morning. It was a minor annoyance compared to the way my young back ached from bending over and picking up the debris left behind from the mower. It was then my job to carry the bigger pieces and load them onto a flatbed trailer attached to the pickup, and at the end of the day, I would unload and stack those same pieces in a different field to be burned some future day.

We sat next to one another when he started huffing air through his nose. Anytime this happened, you knew he had something to say. It was like his own personal tornado siren giving warning of an impending event.

A smile as big as our task at hand exploded across his face and he began speaking while he laughed. "Did I ever tell you about the old man who witnessed a robbery?"

I caught his stare, grinned, and lied. "No, I don't believe I've ever heard that one."

He started almost as if he had never heard my response.

"This old man was on the witness stand when the judge asked him, 'Now are you sure you saw this man rob this man over here?'" Grandpa pointed to an imaginary man in the direction of a stand of trees and another in the opposite direction.

"The old man said, 'Yes sir, that's him right there.'" Grandpa laughed, his voice changing when switching between characters, the judge naturally possessing a voice with more authority.

"The judge then looked at him and said, 'I have a hard time believing that given the distance you were standing from the suspect that you could rightfully accuse this man of committing a crime – nobody's eyes can be that good, just how far can you see?'"

Switching voices back to the witness, he became a little more animated and delivered the punchline. "The old man looked at the judge, puffed up his chest and said, 'I can see all the way to the moon, now just how *fer* is that?'"

I shook my head and found a way to appease him with laughter. At the same time, Grandpa could hardly contain his own joy before he relived the story's ending. He said in a trailing voice, "Yeah, the old man said, 'Now just how *fer* is that?'" Enjoying it all once again.

He quickly changed his demeanor from jester to educator. "You know that story is funny, but it also has something we could all learn from."

Believing it to be nothing more than a silly story I had heard dozens of times, I nodded my head in a disengaging manner without looking at him. But he was undeterred.

"If you think about it, that old man wasn't wrong, he was just looking at things from a different perspective. And, that's true of just about anything. While one person sees it a certain way, another can see it completely different. Neither of them is necessarily wrong, but they both just might be right." He paused for effect.

"Everything in life is how we choose to look at it."

His point was valid, so I agreed. "I can't argue with that."

The conversation turned to me.

"Just how do you see your life?"

My eyebrows arched, and I shrugged my shoulders.

"Take today for example, do you see yourself wasting your time out here picking up sticks, or do you think what you're doing has some meaning or purpose?"

"I guess most days, I just feel lost. I think I should be where my friends are. Going to college, learning about what I'm supposed to be doing with my life. I'm pretty sure picking up sticks wasn't a career choice."

"That's one perspective." He said it as if there was more to tell.

I bit, "What's the other?"

"That what you're doing here today is making a difference. You probably don't see it or believe it but picking up these sticks might help others."

"I just can't see that." It wasn't intended to be argumentative.

"Well think about it," his massive hands palm up now pleading for me to understand, "You clear this field, we raise our cattle, those cattle then feed somebody who might be hungry." It was a point-by-point breakdown. "You just can't possibly know, doing this might keep somebody of importance from starving to death, and then they go on and help more people than me or you can count."

"Maybe," I reluctantly agreed but felt it a bit of a reach.

He dug into the front pocket of the threadbare snap-button shirt he was wearing. Beyond the color, it was indistinguishable from the one he would wear tomorrow. Expertly he twisted the last Winston from its pack, set it between his lips, leaned forward and cupped it between his hands to shield it from the wind as he lit it. He took a long drag, held it, then spoke as smoke escaped in a steady stream following his every word.

"I believe we all have a purpose here, we may not see it, we may not understand it, we may not even agree with it, but there's a meaning to everything we do."

I looked absently to the stand of trees he had gestured to while telling his story about the old man and then responded, "I'm not sure I believe that."

"Well, you should." And, for emphasis, "Because it's true."

"Why? Because God?

"That'd be a fine place to start."

In a single move, he pushed himself from the tailgate, walking away from where I sat, and without looking back, signaling it was time to go back to work.

We finished as much as we could do before breaking for lunch. That afternoon, Grandpa unhitched the trailer in a vacant field where we had been piling the brush for weeks. He left me to unload it, with instructions to pick up any stray sticks in the pasture should I finish before he returned. On that note, he climbed back into the cab of his pickup, waved at me, and left me alone to get started. As I watched him drive out of sight, I picked a long stick from the trailer and chucked it like a fastball in the direction of the burn pile.

I plopped along the ground next to the trailer, my back propped against a rear tire and simmered.

What was I doing?

Why would I be sitting out in a vacant field, under a scorching sun, piling sticks upon a burn pile?

Where were my friends? Enjoying college life, probably playing games of pick-up basketball with their new friends – maybe in front of groups of newly pledged sorority girls.

And here I am stuck in rural Arkansas, where the most exciting thing happening today might be who drove by the tiny Post Office without picking up their mail, and the other 300 people in town wondering why.

I hopped to my feet and started hurling every piece of debris left in trailer to the general direction of the burn pile. By the time my mad fit was over, I had doubled over with exhaustion from the non-stop irrational outburst.

With clenched fists, my head thrown backward, I let out a primal scream born out of frustration. It felt good but was completely childish and totally out of character.

Easing, my open hands found my face, steadying my head as if I was suddenly fearful of losing my mind. I took a deep breath and a few minutes to calm myself.

As the tension disappeared, I briefly considered what Grandpa had sought to teach me earlier in the day. *"I believe we all have a purpose here, we may not see it, we may not understand it, we may not even agree with it, but there's a meaning to everything we do."*

I solemnly stood with my gaze fixed upon an empty trailer. I debated walking home, venturing into my bed, and forgetting that there was more to do. Instead, I turned on my heels, without complaint and began my search for more sticks to add to the growing pile.

CHAPTER ELEVEN

THE MULE

Matthew 25:13 *"Watch therefore, for you know neither the day nor the hour."*

"JUST LIKE THAT FELLOW WHO FOUND THE MULE."

His words came out as they often did, with a smile. It was a wickedly cold day, and nobody could have predicted that in less than six months, he would be dead.

As we sat across from one another at the kitchen table, he looked no worse for wear. Don't get me wrong, cancer was winning, and he was down with two strikes late in the game, but like a batting champ, he kept fouling off cancer's challenges and digging in for the next one.

It was late in the day but far too early to be dark, yet the clouds hovered low and thick blocking out any chance the sun had to shine. My arms folded in front of me, elbows resting on the glossy cherrywood finish, I leaned forward to match his position. A light above the table cast a yellowish glow that seemed to warm the room. Grandma read a book about foods to fight cancer as she sat beneath a reading lamp in the living room. Grandpa and I were posed like two poker players divided by a jackpot, each trying to read the other's bluff.

I finished his statement. "All at once."

He confirmed, "that's how he found it," then softer, "all at once."

My eyes cast downward between us as if I was lamenting the hand I had drawn and realized a jackpot I might not be awarded.

He filled the emptiness with conjecture as he nodded his head while speaking. "Maybe it's better that way. It's something I've been thinking about."

"But then you wouldn't have the opportunity to say goodbye to everyone." I looked him in the eyes and waited for his response.

He unfolded his arms and rubbed his head with both hands. Strands of his thin brown hair appeared and disappeared between the gaps of his fingers. His mouth seemed to clench causing the hollowed valleys of his cheeks to grow deeper. When he finally responded his voice was filled with pain.

"The heck of it is, I think maybe it's worse this way. In most ways, all this time to say goodbye just makes it that much harder."

I responded with a sympathetic nod.

He probed for my opinion. "How would you want to go?"

Truthfully, I had never thought about it. Those thoughts were buried deep.

I never wanted to think about not living.

I loved life. I had experienced a time when I didn't, but now I cherished it, everything about it, and I wasn't ready to acknowledge that my own personal mortality existed. So, I hedged.

"Grandpa, I just don't know. If you're asking me to answer now, I'd say both have pluses and minuses."

"Well, I've had nothing but time to think about it lately." He stopped rubbing his head. "It's worse at night, just being there in the bed and not being able to shut it off."

Now, I shook my head, feeling his hurt.

For a moment neither of us spoke, then he started huffing air through his nose.

"If I got to choose, it'd be better just like the fellow who found the mule." He let the admission linger before continuing. "If it happened all at once, you'd never have to be tortured by knowing it was coming - but not knowing just exactly when – that's been the hardest part."

"I can see that." It was hard to argue with the logic.

"On the other hand, doing it like this, it's giving me a chance to stack up all my worries, get them in order, and be able to let everybody know how much I love them."

"That's maybe the way I'd want it to be for me," I concluded.

He grinned, but it was a joyless expression. "You say that, and I know that sounds good, but it ain't so hot when it's happening to you."

This wasn't an argument that I wanted to engage in, nor was it one for which I could ever be right about. After all, he was the one dodging the sniper living inside his body, and he was the one who was left alone unable to sleep at night as he lay there helpless on a battlefield of tortured thoughts. Who was I to have an opinion about this subject? I immediately wished I could take it back.

"Grandpa, you're right, I'm sorry. I shouldn't have said anything. I can't possibly know which would be better."

"Why are you sorry? I asked you how you wanted to go." He now grinned in a gentle way.

"It's just…" I struggled to say it.

He bravely finished my thought. "It's just, I'm the one dying?"

When he did, the word, *dying,* it struck me hard. Maybe because he said it. Maybe because I didn't want to say it. Probably because I didn't want to face it. I could only muster a weak nod as I struggled to hold back the building pressure behind my eyes.

"It's not the dying that keeps me up at night," he admitted before countering his own words, "Well in a way it is."

I flashed a curious look at him that begged for clarification.

He explained, "The way you live your life, the things you do, the things you wished you had done." The last point dripped with regret.

I interjected carefully. "Grandpa, you've lived a good life, you've told me your amazing experiences, and you're loved by so many."

"All that's true, but when you're dying, none of it was ever enough." It came out as convincing as anything I had ever heard him say. Then he continued, "I'm not so bothered by dying, I've always known that was part of the deal, it's just a matter of wanting to do more before I go."

It wanted to breathe some levity into the conversation. "Ok, when do you want to go deep-sea fishing off the coast of Mexico?"

For a moment it worked.

"I'm ready when you are, let's go," he joked.

Grandma chimed in from the living room, "I'll go find my rod and reel." She said it without ever looking up from her book. Grandpa and I exchanged a smile that seemed to ask in jest, *how do we tell her she's not going?*

He then spoke in a way that indicated the conversation was ending but not before he wrapped it up nicely with a bow.

"Jerrad, I want you to live your life without any regrets. Do everything you want to do and love as big as you can imagine. "

"Take care of your family, be faithful, and never miss a chance to do something you want to do. Even though you'll probably still wish there are things you'd done different – try not to think about that – put your mind on things that make you happy, do everything for the right reason, and give yourself peace."

He paused before finishing.

"… Get yourself to that spot. Do it that way. Be prepared, because you might be like your old grandpa someday, or you might just be like that fellow who found the mule."

CHAPTER TWELVE

Lifted

Isaiah 41:13 *"For I, the Lord your God, hold your right hand; it is I who say to you, "Fear not, I am the one who helps you."*

"I AM SORRY, BUT THEY ARE INSISTING."

At my request, she had asked them to reconsider, but it had fallen on deaf ears.

"It's a bad idea, Mary," I pleaded.

"I might agree, but if you just keep them in the cove, everything should be okay."

I quipped, "Do any of them even know how to canoe?"

Her answer was given with unconvincing eyes and a shrug of her shoulders.

I shook my head in response – nearly seething that we were not bold enough to make the decision for the group. It made little sense to me that we could allow a group of second-grade girl scouts to pile into canoes on such a windy day. From where I stood atop the hill, I could see the whitecaps dancing in a frenzy along the surface of the lake in the canyon below.

I listed off reasonable objections while making one final attempt.

"Mary, I'm begging you. I'll have to wear a jacket down there while supervising. The canoes haven't even been in the water this year. And those kids are way too young to do this even on the best of days."

Mary, my supervisor, was in no mood to continue the discussion. "You better get going, they're outside waiting."

Camp Comeca, a campground where individuals and groups of all ages, associations and faiths gathered for weeklong stays throughout the year. It was my junior year of college, and I was a seasoned staff member at Comeca, in charge of cooking, cleaning, lifeguarding and the supervision of recreational activities – including canoeing.

It was early in the year; the flowers were budding but not bursting. The girl scout group was our first sizable gathering of the season, and they were anxious for outdoor fun. I had tried convincing them of taking a nature hike, playing basketball, or taking a dip in the indoor pool, but they seemed to only have one idea.

A blustery north wind raced across empty farmland into the south canyon where it funneled its way across the lake stirring it in a way only an experienced surfer might enjoy. Down a hill, I led the group of giggling scouts and their teenage counselors from the campgrounds to a cove that offered some wind protection from the canyon-side and a scattering of trees. As we arrived near the water, I gave it one more shot.

Turning to a pair of young counselors, one short and one shorter, both of which were shy of legally driving, I asked, "You sure you want to do this?" Adding, "I think the water is going to be really cold."

They smiled, unknowing, and exuberant. "Yeah, let's do this," the taller of the two was quick to reply.

With that said, I reluctantly readied the canoes and administered the lifejackets and detailed instructions. Then, I asked them a relevant question.

"How many of you have canoed before?" I received no acknowledgment from the group. I took a deep breath – this was getting worse. "How many of you have seen someone use a canoe?"

Of the thirty kids spread between six canoes awaiting departure, one yelled back, "Let's go!" The others quickly voiced their agreement.

I made my way to the six counselors who huddled together awaiting my final instructions, their long hair blowing in the wind, it was hard to disguise their shivering, despite the matching sweatshirts they wore.

I swept my finger from left to right in front of them, "Okay, how many of you have canoed before?"

The one who had spoken before, piped up again, "I mean, I sort of know how to do it. I've seen people do it." I wasn't so sure she had.

She encouraged the others by adding, "I mean, like how hard can it really be, right?"

I measured my thoughts behind covered eyes. I exhaled and hesitated but continued anyway. "Listen," I drew the boundaries of the cove by gesturing with my hand, "you're going to have to stay in this immediate area." I then asked while pointing, "Do you see the area where the water is churning?" The white caps were peeking up at least ten inches in height with no more than an equal distance between them.

The group nodded in unison their expressions clearly lined with worry.

"If you get out there in that area, the canoe could potentially tip over, the water is ice cold, and even though you're wearing a lifejacket, if you go in, you'll swallow a lot of water before I can get you out."

Suddenly the gravity of their unwise choice to go canoeing seemed to set in for most of them. Then the spokesperson of the group once again opened her mouth. "That won't be hard to avoid, let's go. We're ready." The lack of confidence in her voice told a different story.

Regardless of how I felt, the six canoes floated a short distance from where I pushed them from the shore, safely in the confines of the cove, rocking about with their inexperienced and naïve passengers. Many laughs were being shared, a few splashes, and confidence grew within the group. As a result, they began to venture a greater distance from the shoreline.

I sat attentively on the edge of the dock. The wooden structure jutted outward like a splinter stuck in the thumb-like shape of the cove. I struggled to stay warm as the cold wind found its way around the edges of the surrounding geography to ruffle the fabric of my lightweight jacket. Still steaming from Mary's decision and that of the group, I stood to shout a warning to a canoe that started drifting beyond my comfort.

"Hey!" I cupped my hands to amplify my voice. "You need to come back this way!" I started moving both arms demonstrating the direction.

It was useless, they had gone too far. They were headed toward the opening of the cove and had lost complete control of their canoe. The water was too fierce. The wind too strong. The occupants were incapable of changing course. Without regard for my personal safety, I shed my jacket, kicked off my shoes, and dove into the frigid water never considering how challenging it would be to swim while wearing a sweatshirt and jeans.

I cut through the first thirty yards or so of choppy water fueled by raw uninterrupted adrenaline, only to find myself struggling to keep my head above water with no more than ten yards to go. Like a running back seeking a first down against a stingy defense with eleven in the box, I hit a wall, and I was going down.

As my forward momentum stalled, I tried to gasp for air between the intensifying waves of water that seemed to now be arriving against my face one right after the next. Panic started to creep in when my legs, arms, and back began cramping from the frigid waters, my saturated clothes making it increasingly difficult to move. I had swum into danger. No longer protected by the cove, I had entered the body of the lake.

The canoe I had chased held a huddled group of frightened faces, all moving in a violent back and forth motion. They cried with fear for their own lives as well as mine. I shouted for their help when I knew their canoe was beyond my reach.

"Throw me a lifejacket!" It came out as a final hope.

The camp counselor, seeing I was drowning, unlatched the lifejacket from her body and steadied herself before boldly attempting to throw her lifejacket in my direction. It was a sacrificial act that not only showed her selflessness but her remarkable courage as well. Unfortunately, even though it was a relatively short toss, the thieving wind snatched it and took it over her head to the opposite side of the canoe.

My fate had been sealed. I was going to drown. I would be dead in a matter of seconds. My ability to tread in place was quickly fading and each attempt to suck in air between the growing walls of water proved less and less successful. This is where my life would end. I would sink forty feet to the bottom of the lake into a dark abyss.

Would I ever be found?

I understand that it can be a cliché to say *my life flashed before my eyes*. I had also heard others profess it but never knew genuinely what it meant until I found myself alone and broken in the middle of that lake watching a canoe full of young girls, I had tried to save, perilously drift farther away from me. But *flash before my eyes* it did. I witnessed things in a bolt of images chalked full of people, places, things I had experienced and inexplicably those I had not.

Also, I had heard other accounts from those who were resuscitated describe how peaceful their experience with drowning had been. This was something I had never believed. I grew up fearing the water, before learning how to swim and ultimately earning the responsibilities of a lifeguard. Yet, a warm feeling of peace overtook my body.

Resigned to death, to drowning, to never seeing my loved ones again, I sank beneath the surface for the last time. Unable to carry on the fight, unexpectedly something lifted me back to the surface where instinctively my lungs demanded air. I went down once more, but again, was lifted to the surface. Then, again. And, again. Dozens of times - all the while guiding me on a path to shallow waters.

When I crawled the last few feet from the lake that nearly killed me to the edge of the sandy shore, I hurled lake water from my mouth as my gut worked as if it were twisting water from a sponge.

Within a few minutes, the girl scouts appeared and dragged me completely out of the water onto dry land where I crumpled into a sprawled position in the middle of the group, like a bullseye on a target.

They had surrounded me, crying, holding hands, and offering prayers. I scanned the ring of prayer warriors before slipping into a state of unconsciousness, but just before I closed my eyes, I recognized the ones I had tried to save - they appeared to be praying the hardest.

A week or so had passed before I dared to look at the lake again. As I sat on the dock under the light of a warmer sun, I took note of how calm the lake now appeared. *Slick as glass*, that's how my water-skiing friends would have described it. The whole area took on a look of serenity. The colors seemed more vibrant, the air smelled fresher, and I felt more alive than I had ever been.

My thoughts quickly turned to what had happened. I measured the distance from where I sat to the spot in the lake where I had nearly drowned. It was impossible, I thought. How could I have pushed myself back to the surface? The depth of the water in that area of the lake was likely forty, maybe fifty feet deep. How did I have the energy? How did my muscles find a way to work as they seized, cramped, and became unusable?

What happened? Had God intervened? Did God save me like the Trooper believed with my car accident as a teenager?

Was God responsible for the warm feeling I felt and the flash of images of things I recognized as events that I had not yet experienced?

My head began to ache from the mystery. I stood and turned to walk away, before taking one last glance at the lake. Then, I convinced myself with a weak answer - *There must have been a sandbar out there that saved me.*

CHAPTER THIRTEEN

Solo

---

1 Corinthians 13:7 *"Love bears all things, believes all things, hopes all things, endures all things."*

KNOCK. KNOCK. KNOCK. Surprised, I answered the door with a hint of reservation.

"We need to talk." She didn't look at me as the words trembled from her mouth.

Responding to her serious tone, I stepped aside to let her pass by.

Her young face was full of dread and fear for what she needed to tell me. She moved past me without a greeting. The tension was thick as we faced one another while standing inside my cabin. She looked no better than I did as she appeared to have rushed to get ready, while I appeared not to have put forth any effort at all.

She had awakened me. Now, three years into my duties at Camp Comeca, I had learned how and when to nap. On this early afternoon, I had finished my morning chores and sought quiet refuge in my cabin. The art of sneaking in a short snooze before the after-lunch schedule was something I had become quite proficient at accomplishing.

This day was an especially beautiful day. Atop the hill where Comeca could be seen for miles, the earth gave birth to new creations in the forms of budding trees and blossoming flowers. In the valley below, ample rains and periods of sunshine aided the seedlings to break the surface and dot the landscape in perfectly-formed rows. These were surroundings that lived in stark contrast to the way her presence was making me feel.

"You might want to sit down," she said.

I didn't because somehow, I already knew. And at that moment, I wanted to hear it while standing.

She took her own advice while I stood some distance away in a stiff position with my arms folded across my chest. Neither of us seemed to want to look at the other. She buried her head in her hands as she started to speak.

"I'm pregnant." She sounded grieved while at the same time relieved to share her secret.

When she blurted it out, the statement may as well have been a loud whistle blown in a crowded room leaving everyone waiting in silence with angst to hear what might be next.

Mandy had been my girlfriend over my most recent semester. She was dangerously cute and lots of fun. She had also just graduated from high school, and I had recently completed my junior year of college. Shamefully, we were both too young to have been acting like adults for the six months leading up to this moment. Regrettably, we were now left with a very adult situation.

Her unexpected presence had forecasted bad news. We had not frequently spoken in the two weeks since I had left her behind, moving to Comeca after finishing classes. When I had departed school for the summer, there wasn't a clear understanding as to where our relationship stood. Now she sat before me with a helpless stare, as I searched for a way to respond.

She asked, "What are we going to do?"

I took a moment to gather myself by covering my face and turning away from her. The thought crossed my mind that I should just run. Take off and sprint away from the problem. Leave as I had been left by others. But I didn't want that. I couldn't be that. The situation called for courage and compassion.

I finally sat, next to her steadying her shaky hand in mine. I asked her what she wanted to do.

She showed appreciation for my gentle response. After a short time, she calmed and provided her thoughts. "I feel like there are a few options for us." She listed them in order. "We can keep the baby. We can give the baby up for adoption. Or – "

She didn't finish with the third option, but it was understood.

I exhaled and shook my head. "There's only one option."

It appeared to be the answer she was hoping to hear.

We hugged and cried, completely unaware of how challenging the next phase in our lives would be.

Mandy left Comeca that day while I left my camp responsibilities to someone else. I needed some time alone to gather my thoughts. So, I ventured up a hill to the camp's highest point and sat in the shadow of an old wooden cross while I took in the majestic views. As I did, birds flew distantly above the shimmering water twisted between the rocky outcroppings of the canyon below. The sun brilliantly outlined large groups of radiant white clouds that appeared to have been pasted on a magnificent blue background. It was peacefully serene and just the place for me to reflect on my thoughts.

The beautiful setting, the way the sun kissed my skin and the splendor of it all, it could only be the work of God. Painted perfectly as a part of His greatest masterpiece. It felt like the right time and for a fleeting moment, I considered reaching out to Him. Ask Him for wisdom. Pray for Guidance. Seek Advice. *How was I to be a father? How would I provide for this child? What would I say to my family?*

But I ignored the opportunity.

Without further consideration, I pushed myself to my feet and witnessed the brilliance fade away from the sky. The burning source of life slowly sunk beyond the horizon and as the once-vibrant clouds slipped into a darkening canvas.

I moved back down the path from which I arrived – a path littered with confused thoughts lost amidst a hopeless soul who chose to go on his own.

CHAPTER FOURTEEN

Stupidity Gone to Seed

Ephesians 4:32 *"Be kind to one another, tenderhearted, forgiving one another, as God in Christ forgave you."*

"HOW ABOUT YOU DRIVE."

I found his statement to be startling. For I could not recall a time when he had ever yielded in this way, giving up control, offering for anyone else, let alone me, to drive.

It spoke volumes for how he must have been feeling now in the last three months of his life.

"You boys have fun and be careful!" Grandma waved from the doorway as I closed his door after helping him into the pickup.

My grandpa was but a silhouette of what he had been. He no longer possessed the strength or stamina to do common tasks we all take for granted. Cancer was advancing the ball down the field in the final quarter against a battered defense no longer able to hold ground. But, on this day, he wanted to go for a ride, and uniquely, it would be me driving him.

I slowly maneuvered the pickup around the bends in the long driveway and found our way onto the highway. We were headed to Union Hill. No more than a fifteen-minute drive, however, it seemed like an entirely different world – untouched by the modern advances of man.

Along the way we passed open pastures corralled by thinly strung barbed wire, old houses that had been long-abandoned and large forests of trees, so full of leaves, they looked more like clumps of broccoli.

"Turn here," he pointed to a turn I knew all too well.

His instruction made me smile.

"Now just up here, just before the curve you're going to turn again," he directed me and indicated the direction with a long finger.

My smile grew wider.

We turned and rode mostly in silence as the pavement abruptly ended giving way to a poorly maintained red rock road. In no more than a mile, we were inching down a steep hill. At the bottom, a wide creek snaked its way through the overgrowth. The spring waters flowed beneath an old one-lane bridge, the water as transparent as freshly-cleaned glass. He perked up and began to move a little in his seat to gain a better view.

"Stop right here." He motioned for me to pull off onto the side of the road just past the bridge to an area not made for parking.

"You sure I'm off the road enough?" I asked.

He smiled and answered, "I don't think you'll have to worry about seeing anybody else."

It was that kind of place. Somewhere lost in time, where some people used to be and now where very few would ever be.

I helped his weakened body out of the truck and over to the edge of the water. He pulled a Winston from his pocket and held it unlit and hid it in his hand while he spoke as he surveyed familiar surroundings.

"We caught a lot of fish outta here." He took a moment to relish in the memory.

"Cane poles, a few worms, it wasn't nothing to spend all day down here when I was kid. And when we got tired of fishing, we'd go in for a swim."

I stood with my hands in the pockets of my jeans, next to him, enjoying his moment. I felt like we were the only two people in the world as we stood creek-side on an early spring day under the bluest of skies. It could have been 1940 as easily as 2016, and nothing around us would have indicated otherwise.

As if he was remembering a long-ago secret his face erupted into a wide smile.

"One time, me and Arthur were down on the creek swimming," his laughing caused him to cough and pause but only for a second.

"And a big old ugly water snake got to chasing him," his laugh coming between each breathy word, "and boy, he jumped out of the water and took off running back to the house never so much as looking over his shoulder, just like that snake was chasing him the whole way. And I just laughed and laughed – thought I never would stop laughing. Him running from that snake just like it was striking at his heels, every time his feet hit the ground."

Arthur was his older brother, there were two more brothers, also older, Grandpa had been the youngest but undoubtedly the biggest prankster. They all grew up near this creek in a general area called Union Hill. Since I was old enough to remember I had heard endless stories about the trials and shenanigans of my grandpa and his brothers.

"You know for a little while, Arthur was mad at me about that snake. I'd tease him about it every time we came back down to the creek." Grandpa still found this to be funny. "I'd say, Arthur, I sure hope that mean old ugly snake doesn't get to chasing you." His signature laugh made an appearance before he continued. "Arthur, he'd puff at me and tell me where to go – oh, it made me laugh. I never would let him forget about it."

He then admitted. "Truth is, I'd ran just like he did!"

"I might be mad at you, too," I teased.

"Well, if you'd be mad forever, that'd be a long time."

He nodded with every word and then grinned at his own wisdom.

Finally, he lit his cigarette, inhaled, and blew toxins into the air away from me. He found a large flat rock to sit on and looked at me with a thoughtful glance before sitting down. I found a nearly identical rock and eased along beside him.

"I hope you're not still mad at anybody." His voice striking a more sentimental chord.

"What makes you say that?"

"I know you might feel like you could be. Maybe even ought to be."

We both stared at the water as it cascaded along bigger rocks in shallower portions of the creek.

He continued, "Your momma and daddy always loved you. Whatever happened when you were a kid, there's no need to be mad about it forever – because if you're mad forever that'd be a long time."

He looked back to me and smiled. "Forgiveness is a powerful thing. It's not easy and not everyone can do it. But you can." The last part he emphasized with a deeper tone.

I picked up a small flat rock lying beside me, and I skipped it onto the surface of the water. "Grandpa, I suppose you're right, but some things just can't be forgotten."

He responded, "I didn't say forget. I said forgive." He said the word louder to make sure I heard it clearly. "There's a big difference in the two. You don't have to forget anything that's ever happened in your life. Your experiences make you who you are. But when you forgive somebody, you're choosing not to hold those experiences you don't like against them. Forgiveness is about understanding and looking past all your grievances. Life is way too short to hold grudges."

He inhaled a massive amount of nicotine from his cigarette, studied it and flicked it into the water while forcing the last remnants of smoke to pour out from his lungs.

"Grandpa, did you ever hold any grudges?"

"Yeah, I did." It came out slow, full of remorse.

"Sounds like maybe you regret that."

He was quick to reply. "I do, and it's what I'm trying to help you understand." He turned his body in my direction and spoke while pleading with his hands. "If you get mad at somebody, hold that against them - you'll never get all that time back that could have been spent enjoying each other. Instead, we let some little thing get between us and decide we're better off being mad."

He studied me before finishing with a stern warning. "It's stupidity gone to seed."

Then, he picked up a small rock and tossed it into the water.

"Besides that, either you or they may run out of time before you can make it right."

His words were meaningful but came out as an afterthought.

I nodded and turned away to hide my thoughts, listening to his wisdom.

"You'll be better for it by just loving those who love you. Give people a second chance, enjoy your life and die without any regrets or grudges."

I wasn't convinced, but agreed, "It all sounds good."

"It is good. The Bible says we're supposed to forgive, love one another."

I quipped, "Sometimes forgiveness is hard to give."

With that, I stood to my feet and offered a helping hand to lift him from the rock. Stubbornly, he struggled and pushed himself up straight all the while grinning with a sense of accomplishment before stating, "Hard ain't no step for a *Stepper*."

CHAPTER FIFTEEN

Skittish

Proverbs 3:5 *"Trust in the Lord with all your heart, and do not lean on your own understanding."*

"DON'T BE LIKE THE WOMAN WORRIED ABOUT THE HAM." It wasn't a perfect fit for the situation, but I understood.

"You know how she lived her life?" He asked knowing that I did.

"I do."

"Well then, if you don't move on from this, you'll live your whole life like that woman who spent all her time watching that hanging ham, worried it might fall on somebody."

I mockingly asked, "Did that woman get divorced, too?"

"She may have." He joked but it fell flat.

"Grandpa, I feel like I've failed. I never wanted this for my life – for Mandy's life. I never wanted my daughter to be from divorced parents like me. Now, here I am." I lamented.

"Jerrad, you can choose to be whatever kind of parent you want to be. This ain't the way anybody wanted it to be, but now you got to pull yourself up by your britches and get on about your business."

"Okay," I managed to muster a response.

"Now how you choose to go about your business is up to you. You've got everything you need to move on and make the best of this. So, do you want to believe that things will be alright, or do you want to sit around and worry about things you ain't got a bit of control over?"

I agreed, made an excuse to get off the phone and then sat there wishing he wasn't ten hours away. I needed a hug – to be in his presence. Not even 25 years old and I had already failed at being a husband, but I made a promise to myself that I wasn't going to fail at being a father.

After Mandy knocked on my door and delivered the news, we were exchanging our vows in front of family and friends by the end of the summer. Within six months, we would be the parents of a beautiful daughter, Hannah. Before our baby took her first step, we separated, then divorced.

There's not a singular reason I can point to as to why our marriage didn't work. Outside of being too young and having rushed into marriage, we also struggled financially as I finished up school while Mandy worked the register at her grandpa's grocery store. It was an unfortunate combination of circumstances that led to our decision to move in opposite directions, however, we did so with Hannah as our focus.

Being a good dad to my daughter, Hannah, became my primary focus. Mandy and I formed a friendship and shared in the successes and failures of our daughter's young life. I was determined to make it work in every way possible.

My first teaching job was nearby so that I could remain present in Hannah's life. We spent weekends, Wednesday nights and every other holiday together. Because of our combined efforts, Hannah experienced a childhood with two parents who loved her without pause, who helped shape her with a strong moral compass.

Proudly, I had been present and purposeful in Hannah's life. And sometime after her tenth birthday, Grandpa expressed his pride for her and for me.

I had returned to Arkansas for a visit. Woke to the sounds of birds singing outside my bedroom window and the smells of a homecooked breakfast. After we all gathered around the table to share generous portions of bacon and eggs, Grandpa asked me to sit with him on the front porch.

Grandpa cradled a chunky mug filled with coffee as we sat in familiar positions. The rich aroma filled the space as we looked upon the late-morning sunshine darting between trees, checkering the ground with shadows. He sipped from his coffee and seemed to savor the goodness of it all before sharing his thoughts.

"I'm proud of Hannah," he said it with profound sincerity.

"Me, too." I looked over my shoulder through the window to see Hannah smiling and talking to Grandma as they sat next to one another on the sofa in the living room.

"She sure has turned out good. You and Mandy ought to be proud of how you're raising her."

"Mandy more than me, but I'll take the praise." I deflected to Mandy because she was the custodial parent while I mostly played the role of weekend dad.

He laughed and acknowledged that I was probably right.

"Either way, I'm proud of you."

"Thanks, Grandpa." It filled me with joy to know that he was proud.

"It would've been easy for you and Mandy to have gotten crossways with one another. If you had, Hannah would've suffered and probably wouldn't have turned out so good."

"It hasn't always been easy, but we always try to keep what's best for Hannah at the forefront of every decision we make together."

"And that's the way it ought to be," he concurred.

A slinky black cat with a skittish demeanor slid around my grandpa's legs.

"Hello, *Tom*." He couldn't have said it any kinder as he leaned forward and gently stroked *Tom's* back. The poor-looking cat purred in delight and arched his back impossibly high in response to the attention.

Every stray male cat that had ever shown up on that porch was given the name, *Tom* unless he was black, for which there was a chance he would be called *Blackie*, while every female cat, regardless of color was to be named, *Momma*. Despite such an amazing imagination, Grandpa apparently was never very creative when it came to naming cats.

"Jerrad, just look at *Tom*," Grandpa was hunched over rubbing the cat with a big hand.

I laughed and admitted, "He's scared to death of me."

"Oh, he's a dandy." And just as quickly as the cat appeared, he darted away. Bounding down the front steps as if his feet never touched the ground. Swiftly, in a mad instant, he was gone.

Grandpa got a kick out of it and laughed with bright eyes as he watched *Tom* hot foot it around the corner of the house.

"Tom's a lot like people." He sat straight again in his chair, took another sip from his coffee.

"Crazy?" I asked rhetorically.

"Nah, he's not crazy. He's just not real trusting. Somebody did something bad to him… I suspect they hit him with a broom - every time he sees a broom he runs for the hills." He shook his head with genuine sympathy. "But Tom, if he's ever gonna be happy again, he's got to realize that not everybody will treat him that way — and not every broom will be used to hit him."

"Are you talking about me when you say, *people?*"

"You're sure enough cracker-jack smart." He grinned. "I'm not exactly talking about you, but yeah, it applies. You've got to start trusting again."

"Are you giving me dating advice?" I grinned.

"I'm giving you living advice." He countered.

"Okay." I tried to respect what he said.

"Give somebody a chance. Allow yourself to trust, and you might just find you'll be happier than you could ever imagine."

I nodded and thanked him for his thoughtfulness.

He responded with a kind look.

Then he leaned forward to the edge of his chair and pointed with his coffee cup to the yard where *Tom* was racing back in our direction. With perfect timing, Grandpa boasted with a triumphant expression.

"See there, *Tom's* pretty smart, too."

CHAPTER SIXTEEN

Time Paused

Deuteronomy 32:7 *"Remember the days of old; consider the years of many generations; ask your father, and he will show you, your elders, and they will tell you."*

"SO MUCH OF IT LOOKS THE SAME AS IT ALWAYS DID."

I heard him say it like he wanted it to be true.

Just a short distance from the creek, we pulled off the main road and crept along a bumpy driveway. Beyond the short path, sitting behind a clump of trees, Grandpa studied his childhood home and its surroundings.

He started huffing air through his nose in a way that made it clear that his brain was processing thoughts and memories at a rapid pace as we slowly drew closer. While he couldn't break his stare fixed on the old weathered dwelling of his youth, I couldn't help but look at him with loving admiration wondering what his magnificent mind must be thinking at that moment. So many of the stories I had heard were staged on these grounds, played out with colorful characters who had long since passed. Now in the final passages of his life, he was back to relive it all.

Time seemed to have ignored this place by choice. A simple box-shaped house with faded shingles and peeling paint rested solemnly in the shade of Oak and Elm, an open grassy field spread wide and bright behind the house, and a line of trees at the back of the field hid the deer woods and Old Man Bear's Cave.

This wasn't my first time coming here with Grandpa, but I realized it would be our last. That thought alone placed the details of it all into a different realm. It was an experience where nostalgia invaded and conquered all my senses. I fought back the emotions of the moment and did my best to stay strong.

As I parked, Grandpa spilled out of the pickup, lifted his pants back to his hips, and stood in place, gazing around like he was seeing it and falling in love with it for the very first time. He started talking as I took to his side. I offered a hand of support to help him steady himself upon weakened legs – which he proudly declined.

"Seems like yesterday," he gestured toward the house with his hand, "I was running around this yard, no shoes, no shirt, not a care in the world." His eyes suddenly grew misty.

He looked at me and placed his hand upon my shoulder. "It goes like the blink of an eye."

I nodded to agree. The moment was his, and I didn't intend to interrupt.

"I never could have dreamed that life would happen so fast. As I look around this place," his watery eyes now drifting back to view his childhood surroundings, "I can still see myself as a young boy." He started to choke up, before suppressing his emotions. "I see Momma, Daddy, all my brothers."

I placed my hand on top of his which remained on my shoulder. Hard to say if his was there for affection or for support, either way, I embraced him for it.

"In the end, the only thing that really matters is family. It's the love and memories of family that I'm most proud of. No amount of money or collection of things will mean a dadburn thing if you didn't make memories with your family - if you didn't love each other - if you can't have all that in your heart when it's time to go, then you'll leave this earth with what you came with. Nothing at all."

A brief silence fell softly between us. While I pondered the magnitude of his profound statement, I listened to the wind rustle the leaves and swoosh the tall grass. The afternoon sun brought warmth to my skin, and a feeling of peacefulness engulfed my body replacing the stirring of emotions. I wanted to push the pause button on life and stay in this place until a time of my choosing. When my Grandpa's hand would rest upon my shoulder and my hand would rest upon his. There would be no advancement of cancer. No real-world responsibilities. Only a grandfather and his grandson reminiscing in a place time had forgotten.

Remembering something important, Grandpa pointed to a specific direction behind the house. "We used to have an old momma cat, she lived out there in the hollow of that tree. One winter she kept us all alive. If it hadn't been for her, we'd have all starved to death. That winter, we ate water gravy for breakfast, lunch, and dinner. We didn't have any meat and wasn't having a bit of luck when we went hunting for it. Then one day that momma cat brought a rabbit up on the porch and left it by the door. Then nearly every day she'd catch a rabbit and bring them to the door there for us to fetch. How she knew we needed em', I'll never know… She saved us, that old momma cat."

"Let's go for a walk," he said and weakly stepped away from the pickup.

I obliged and walked beside him with a careful eye.

He pulled a Winston from his front pocket but didn't light it. He carried it in his hand and continued his final trip down memory lane.

"It's hard for me to believe that life can happen so fast." It was a point he found hard to let go of given where we were. "And the older you get the faster it goes. When I was a kid, the days seemed so long – never did think the day would end. Ain't been that way ever since I started getting old."

It prompted a question from me.

"Looking back, would you do anything different?" I asked.

He nodded, and I waited for him to elaborate.

"For one thing, I'd took care of myself a little better." He crumpled the unlit cigarette he had been holding and tossed it to the ground. "Wished I never had started smoking those things."

I forced a smile and rubbed his back as we stood looking down to the ground where he had thrown the Winston.

"I guess other than that, I don't really have a whole lot I'd change. Things turned out pretty good." He looked from the ground back to the house and smiled. "It was tough when I was growing up, but we didn't know it was tough. It was just…" He held out a hand looking for a way to explain it. I filled in the blank.

"Life," I interjected.

"That's it. It was just life. We worked hard. Ate what we could, when we could. Did what we had to do to survive. But we didn't know any better for it. It was just life." The last word was said as if he was satisfied with how a single word described it all.

Once again, he placed his hand on my shoulder, looked at me, but this time his eyes were bright, and he started laughing.

"What?" I genuinely didn't know where this was coming from.

His answer was nearly inaudible as he tried to get it out through his growing laughter.

"You remember," his voice interrupted by a violent coughing spell, "... when I showed you Old Man Bear's Cave?" When he finally got it out, he alternated between coughing and laughing.

I answered him with a look that indicated I'd rather not talk about it.

Just a few years back, Grandpa had driven me to this exact same place. Along the drive, he peppered me with stories about the great bear that lived along the bluffs at the edge of the woods. He detailed encounters he and his brothers experienced while growing up. The entire charade was to build my anxiety about the legendary beast. As we arrived and walked across the open field toward the tree line, he assured me that Old Man Bear was long dead.

"Nah, I'm pretty sure he died years ago. But the cave is still there, and you're gonna want to see it. I wouldn't even begin to think about going down there if I thought he might still be there... Surely, we'll be alright"

Wondering, I wandered along in his footsteps as my conscious mind drifted into a stream of thoughts about the great bear that used to occupy this territory.

"Oh, I wished you could have seen that old bear. Biggest bear you could ever have imagined. You didn't dare go near his cave. He'd stand up on his hind legs and roar – make every hair on the back of your neck stand straight. I suppose some paid the price for getting too close

The Stepper

to his home, but we always knew better than to go messing around his place."

Grandpa's warning didn't go unnoticed.

We eased past the edge of the woods. Grandpa led the way down a rocky slope. A few yards to our left an outcropping of rocks caught my vision. He turned and looked at me and motioned with his hand and spoke in a hushed tone.

"Right on around that corner is where you'll find Old Man Bear's Cave."

He pressed on, and I followed a cautionary distance behind him. When we got to the outcropping, he moved around the side of it just beyond my view. Then, just as I attempted the same route around the rocks, I found that Grandpa had turned back and was now facing me with bulging eyes, and he shouted with what I believed to be fear.

"Run! Run! It's a bear! Run!"

I didn't hesitate, spun on my heels and took off in an instant. When I reached an embankment a few steps from the outcropping, I lost my footing, slipped and fell, all the while, continuing to spin my wheels with sheer panic. It was then that I glanced back to see if the bear was closing in on me.

I had imagined that Old Man Bear was about to have me for lunch, instead, I witnessed Grandpa leaning against the outcropping,

100

his patented laugh on full display, hardly able to stand as his body was disabled with laughter.

Now as we stood here near the house, merely a few seconds removed from something deeply nostalgic and philosophical, Grandpa was showcasing that same level of laughter. I shook my head and laughed at myself.

"Grandpa, you know you set me up for that. You made me believe Old Man Bear was going to attack me."

"You didn't even care about your poor old Grandpa, just took off and left me," His words cloaked by laughter.

"I guess I figured I didn't need to outrun the bear, just outrun you, and I'd be okay."

He enjoyed my response.

After settling on that idea, his joy quickly faded, and a serious look replaced his smile.

"I think we'd better go back to the truck."

It was difficult for me to see him surrender and it pained me to know how much he must have been hurting.

I helped him back to the truck. As he maneuvered onto the seat, he fought for a deep breath and then exhaled as if to indicate he could do no more. When I moved around behind the wheel, I acknowledged this and told him we were headed back home. In reaction to this, he reached across the length of the cab and squeezed my hand and manufactured a smile.

"Before we do, I've got one more place I want to show you."

CHAPTER SEVENTEEN

AT FIRST SIGHT

---

1 John 4:18 *"There is no fear in love, but perfect love casts out fear. For fear has to do with punishment, and whoever fears has not been perfected in love."*

"I'D SAY YOU'VE WAITED LONG ENOUGH."

Grandpa liked Julia and teased me for waiting so long to ask her to be my wife.

"Grandpa, I think she was starting to feel the same way."

"How long has it been?"

"It's been around five years."

"You ought to know by now."

"I knew it from the first time I saw her."

"What took you so long?"

"Good question. I guess I wanted to be sure."

"Thought you was sure the first time you saw her?"

"I was."

He laughed and called for Grandma, "Momma, Jerrad's on the phone. He's got something he wants to tell you. He thinks he's sure about it."

Grandpa congratulated me, laughed some more and handed the phone to Grandma.

"Hello, Angel!"

"Hello, Grandma."

"What's this I hear that you've got something to tell me about?"

"I'm going to ask Julia to marry me."

"Well, Okay! It's about time."

"So, I've heard."

"Now, just how long has it been?"

"Around five years."

She giggled. "Well, you could have been like your grandpa."

"How's that?"

She giggled again and sounded as happy as a tickled child.

"When Norm was in the Navy out in San Diego, he was stationed with my brother, Lloyd. Me and mom lived in a little old apartment. One night, Lloyd brought your grandpa home with him for dinner. We had heard stories about Norm, but this was the first time meeting him."

"What did you think of him?"

"Oh, he was charming, and boy was he good looking. He was tall, slender, and tan. Had those blue eyes and that big grin. He looked like trouble in a good way."

"He must have found you attractive as well."

She laughed and quickly responded with modesty. "Well, I don't know about that. Here I was cooking all day getting ready for the dinner. My hair was up in a bun. My clothes were filthy. I looked pitiful."

She paused as if she was picturing it all in her mind again before she continued.

"Anyway, we went to a dance that night. We danced and had a good time. Before the dance was over, Norm had asked me to marry him." She laughed at the silliness of it all.

"No kidding?"

"Honest, that's just the way it happened."

"Wow. Now that's love at first sight."

"It was for him." She teased and giggled.

"What took me so long?"

"I'm sure Julia was asking herself the same question."

Julia Jane Lebedz, the love of my life. A woman who was everything I wanted, but more importantly, everything God knew I needed. I knew the moment I saw her, if she would go for it, I'd spend the rest of my life by her side. When my eyes first met hers, I found it impossible to disengage. She made me want to be better, do better and be more. I had never met anyone more beautiful with a heart so full of love, compassion and empathy for others.

When I finally got the nerve to propose, she broke down in tears and said something to the effect that, *it's about time or finally.* Whatever she said, it was accurate. I had waited a long time. After previously bringing a child into the world and then making that same child, who I loved more than anything, a child who would grow up with divorced parents, I was determined to never repeat those actions. Lucky for me, Julia had been patient with me, and, Julia, who also loved Hannah, wanted children of her own.

In December of 2012, Julia gave birth to our oldest son, Jackson. He was Grandpa's birthday present as he was nearly born on the same day. Jackson, Jack as we call him, became the center of our universe. We doted over him as new parents do, took endless pictures and posted them on Facebook, answered his every cry. He became our everything. Someday, I'm sure we'll hear about it from our other children when they are old enough to notice the discrepancy in the number of pictures taken for each of them.

Grandpa immediately took a considerable liking to Jack. We frequently visited my grandparents in Arkansas. From the time he was an infant, Grandpa would put Jack on his lap and rock him in his big chair. As Jack grew older, they watched movies together on the iPad and played together with toys. With Jack, Grandpa let his softer side be seen without any barriers.

In-between visits, when Jack was old enough to ask for Grandpa, we made it routine to call him using the iPad so that he and Jack could Facetime one another. During their weekly video visits, Jack would babble and bring toys to show him. Grandpa would brag about the toys and the two of them would share laughter and some type of language that only they were privy to understanding.

The love between Grandpa and Jack was instant and deep.

CHAPTER EIGHTEEN

Someplace Nice

Matthew 11:28 *"Come to me, all who labor and are heavy laden, and I will give you rest."*

"HERE'S WHERE THE OLD POST OFFICE USED TO BE."

We had driven more than a mile from the homestead and he continued to see reminders along the roadway from his childhood.

I asked, "So, this is where you picked up the radio?"

"Oh, we were so excited. Me and Arthur nearly ran the whole way to the post office to get it. Then we took turns carrying it all the way home. The case was so heavy, oh it was heavy, but the battery was heavier than you could have ever imagined. If we hadn't been so happy about it, we might have ditched it and went on pretending we never saw it."

He seemed to perk up in his seat as he fondly relived the memory.

"When we got it home, all of us gathered around it, looking at it like we just couldn't hardly wait to hear it work. We cranked on it to get the battery going and not a single one of us could help but smile when we heard voices come through the speaker."

I imagined his smile then as I was seeing it now.

"My favorite program was a scary program. It came on after dark. I'd work all day thinking about it and couldn't wait to get home to listen to it. My imagination would run wild hearing the sounds and just thinking about what would happen next."

"That's a great memory," I said.

"It really was."

He pointed to another landmark.

"Over there's where I went to school."

"And you walked to school?"

"Every day."

"Wow, that's a long walk and it really is uphill both ways."

He grinned.

"My teacher rode a horse, all the way over here from Pleasant Plains, rain or shine. We just had a little one-room schoolhouse. I didn't get to go for too long, but he was a good teacher. When I got older, I stopped going on the account I had to work instead."

"Kids don't realize how easy they have it today," I stated.

"No, and I hope that's not a problem someday." He expressed genuine concern.

The road we had been traveling on ended, and we turned left onto a highway shaded by trees on both sides. We had only been on it a short distance before we reached a roadside church hidden in the shadows of towering trees. The church was a modest and unremarkable building made of long boards painted white. We followed a small earthen road that curved around the side of the church. Hidden behind the small place of worship was a cemetery. Grandpa pointed in the direction he wanted me to go and directed me to stop when we had arrived at our destination.

"Right here," he said.

His plot, purchased next to another reserved for Grandma, sat upon a small green hill set in a tranquil area near the back corner of the acreage.

Quietly, we walked together toward the plots.

"This is it."

There was a tinge of trepidation in his voice.

I commented, "It's a beautiful place."

I didn't know exactly how to respond. But it truly was one of the most serene places I had ever visited. On this day, the weather was perfect, the freshly cut grass boasted a deep green color contrasted against the light blue sky above, the air so quiet that even the birds seemingly respected the peaceful nature of the solemn ground.

"Look over yonder." He whispered it as he looked down the length of his arm as it extended from his body, like a hunter lining up a shot through a scope.

He had pointed to a young deer in the distance just in front of a line of trees along the back of the sacred ground. The deer suddenly acted as if it was an uninvited witness to our conversation and had been caught listening-in, thus its eyes grew wide, body stiffened, and ears stood upward. We watched it momentarily, before it bounded off and disappeared into the darkness of the forest.

"Wasn't she pretty?" He asked rhetorically.

"Beautiful." And, she was.

"You know, I have loved animals my whole life. Whether it was a deer or a squirrel, I've always seen something good in all of them."

This was true, from random opossums to raccoons that would show up at Grandpa's back door, he was always feeding them and caring for their needs.

"I hate to leave this world and all that I've enjoyed."

"This world is going to miss you as well." It came out naturally.

"Not too long from now, I'll be right there in the ground." He nodded to an open grass spot that would occupy his remains in less than three months. "But I don't really believe it'll be me in the ground there."

The thought of him lying beneath the ground paralyzed me. I could barely breathe, let alone speak.

He seemed to recognize this and introduced some levity.

"Did I ever tell you about the old man who died?"

I smiled and shook my head.

"Well, this old man, he died. Everybody he left behind was boo-hooing and carrying on. They had a big funeral. The wife and all the old man's kids were there. The preacher gave a big speech, and everybody cried again..."

He coughed a little before controlling it to continue.

"...When they took the old man to the cemetery to bury him, they all reached for the casket afraid to let him go. Through all of it, the old man sat there with God watching from above.

After they shoveled the last bit of dirt on the casket, the old man looked at God and said to him, 'It makes me sad to see everyone crying for me.' Then God looked at the old man, laughed and told him, 'They're not crying for you because you're dead. They're crying because you've gone on to someplace nice and left them all behind.'"

Grandpa held my stare as he grinned from ear to ear. I tried my best to match him.

"Jerrad, don't be sad about this. One way or another this is how it was supposed to be. Don't think of it as me dying but think of it as me going someplace else."

"Someplace nice?" I asked.

"I hope so," he quickly replied with a smile. "As people I loved have passed on, they live on inside my heart and my memories. They never did really die. I've shared some of those people and their stories with you. Maybe they'll keep on living when you keep telling about them. The point is, I'll always be here so long as you and others go on thinking about me. So, in some way, I'll keep on living even after my body goes in the ground."

I reached for him and wrapped him in a hug – savoring the way he felt, smelled, looked. I stood there holding him realizing how much stronger he was than me. How much wiser he was than I could ever be. How unprepared I was to let him go.

When I finally eased away from him, releasing him from my embrace, I looked him in the eyes and told him, "I love you."

His eyes glistened, and his mouth started with a tremble, then he grinned at me and said, "I love you, too."

CHAPTER NINETEEN

SOON

JOHN 14:1-3 *"Let not your hearts be troubled. Believe in God; believe also in me. In my Father's house are many rooms. If it were not so, would I have told you that I go to prepare a place for you? And if I go and prepare a place for you, I will come again and will take you to myself, that where I am you may be also."*

"JERRAD, HE'S NOT DOING WELL."

My aunt Beverly had told me that Grandpa had become bedridden and was losing his battle to the hateful disease with each breath. I was driving and would be arriving the next day. But somehow, I felt late.

When I finally arrived from Nebraska, nothing could have prepared me for what I was about to see. While, I knew that he had steadily digressed from my last visit with Hannah just three weeks earlier, the changes were overwhelmingly dramatic.

Now too weak to stand or able to eat or drink without the help of others, the site of the man who always seemed so strong shocked me. I cried as soon as I saw him, my hand covering my mouth.

When I walked into the room, he appeared to be sleeping flat on his back with his hands folded atop his chest. His eyes were closed, and he did not move. His airway sounded obstructed, and he seemed to be fighting for each breath. Lung Cancer had infiltrated too deep and would soon force his surrender. It was painfully obvious to me - Grandpa was no longer playing offense.

My aunt Beverly moved to my side and rested her head on my shoulder while interlocking her arms around one of mine. "I'm so glad you're here." She said it with a soft and caring voice. Beverly, such a loving, kind and passionate individual. Nobody ever loved their daddy more.

She was tired, and I suppose she dreaded what was to come. They were all tired. My grandma, dad, and Beverly had been attending to Grandpa's every need around the clock for days on end and it was starting to wear them down. Any little help I could provide would certainly be welcomed. But more than that, at a time like this, it's reassuring to have family around to lean on.

It was Grandpa's choice to die at home. He didn't want to be taken to the hospital to pass. Therefore, Grandma, Beverly, and my dad made sure his final weeks at home were made comfortable. Hospice provided as much assistance as they could, but it was mostly up to the family to care for him at the end. It was a courageous undertaking by the three of them. One can never be fully prepared for the physical and emotional toll taken on those who are tasked with spoon-feeding, assisting bathroom needs, and swabbing strings of mucus from a loved one's mouth.

"Is he hurting?" I asked Beverly.

She used one hand to lovingly stroke my arm. "I don't know. He won't take any pain medicine, but then again, he doesn't complain. I'm sure he's hurting, but he's not letting anyone know it."

I leaned my head toward hers resting on my shoulder. "I hate this."

She did, too. We all did.

"Daddy's going to be glad to see you when he wakes up," she said.

"Hope he recognizes me."

"Oh yeah, he's still got his mind about him for the most part."

I turned to her and squeezed her with both arms wrapped tightly around her. I suddenly felt helpless, hopeless.

When he finally woke, I moved by his side, sat on the side of the bed and said hello. I put my hand on his arm and greeted his face with a smile.

"Hello, Jerrad." He sounded hoarse and mustered a thin grin.

"Hello, Grandpa." I leaned down and kissed him on the forehead. "Don't we have something better to do than lay around this house all day?" I teased.

"I suppose we do," he obliged.

"How are you feeling?"

"Pretty tolerable like, thank you." He was lying but tried to sell it with a faint smile.

"Anything I can do for you?"

"Can you get me a cigarette?" I couldn't tell if he was joking or not.

"I'll see what I can do." I was joking.

With that, he winced and asked for some help by motioning to the others in the room. He needed to relieve himself and needed help.

Over the next four days and nights, he faded quicker than I could have anticipated. The disease not only wrecked his physique, but it also impacted his mind. He was beginning to show signs of worry, hallucinations, imagining things that weren't really happening. He teetered between being too hot and too cold, could no longer swallow, and the worst of it, his breathing became more and more labored with every attempted breath.

"I don't know how much longer he can hang on," I said to my dad.

"I don't either, but I don't want him to suffer anymore." He said it with great sadness, his eyes full of worry.

My dad and I stayed up through most of the night by his side. I was sure it would be his last. It wasn't. The next day I had to leave for work. I hated to go, but it was unavoidable, my attendance necessary. I would be back in four days, but for him to hold on until then would take a miracle. I kneeled by his bed, took his cold hand in mine and, said goodbye. As I spoke, he turned his head and looked at me through heavy eyes. My words came out in a whisper - strong in the beginning but quickly fell to pieces.

"Grandpa, I have loved you so much. You have taught me how to love, how to live, and how to be a good person. I will forever remember you for those things. But I will also remember you for your spirit, your humor, and the kind ways you helped me learn how to do just about everything I know how to do. If not for you, I wouldn't be half the man I am today."

I dropped my head onto my hand as I held his hand a little tighter. I could no longer hold back the growing pressure behind my eyes. When the dam broke, forty plus years of loving emotion spilled from my eyes, my body heaving with grief. I shook my head as teardrops continued rolling down my face. I choked back the pain to look at him again, only to see that he too was crying.

My head moved back and forth as I looked into his eyes for what I knew to be the last time. Rivers of tears cascaded along my cheeks, my lips stretched tightly straight across my face to barricade the deep cry desperate to escape. It took a herculean effort to produce any final words. When it came out, my voice cracked, wobbled, and I couldn't even be sure he heard me.

"I'll be back in four days...I want to see you, again... But, if I can't...I want you to know that it's okay to go...Don't fight it...It's okay......I love you Grandpa - I'll always love you."

His eyes squeezed shut, tears pooled at the corners, he whispered, . "Love you...See you soon."

I leaned forward and kissed him on the forehead – this time it was goodbye.

CHAPTER TWENTY

REFLECTIONS

Ecclesiastes 3:1-15 *"For everything there is a season, and a time for every matter under heaven: a time to be born, and a time to die; a time to plant, and a time to pluck up what is planted; a time to kill, and a time to heal; a time to break down, and a time to build up; a time to weep, and a time to laugh; a time to mourn, and a time to dance; a time to cast away stones, and a time to gather stones together; a time to embrace, and a time to refrain from embracing; ...*

"SEE YOU SOON."

It was a phrase Jack had adopted from Mickey Mouse and used frequently. Grandpa used it in conversation with Jack, and before we knew what had happened, it was pretty typical for us to say, "See you soon," instead of goodbye.

Now, pausing in my truck at the end of the driveway, I peered into the rearview mirror to see the house perfectly framed in the reflection. The house on the hill. The long white-rocked driveway that led to the front porch that was instrumental in raising me. All of it sat reflected in the mirror, unchanged, and yet, I feared it would never be the same. *How would I ever make my way up this drive again knowing he wasn't there waiting with those loving, open arms?*

That porch reminded me of childhood days where Grandpa would tease me about wolves and panthers living in the dark shadows paralleling the long driveway. Late in the evenings when I wasn't staying overnight, I would have to run down the drive, dash across the road, and sprint to the front door of the old white house where I lived. On every occasion, just before Grandpa cracked his own front door, he offered a final warning.

"Now, don't let that old wolf get you." His eyes wide with a frightful expression.

Most often Grandma would sternly and quickly rebuke his efforts to scare.

"Norman Earl!" She made the *Earl* sound longer than the *Norman*. "Don't you do that to that boy. You'll get him run over on that road by scaring him like that."

It rarely deterred him from carrying on – and she had to know her rebuke wouldn't do a thing other than fuel his laughter.

Each time I stepped onto the front porch to begin my journey home, Grandpa would flick on the porch light illuminating the first few steps of my mad dash in a yellow-orange haze.

"That old wolf might be out there — don't let him get you," he warned again but this time in a quieter way as to not be heard by Grandma.

With that, I would take off from the porch in a full sprint, never looking back, holding my breath the entire way.

Meanwhile, Grandpa would stand at the door, flicking the light, and ushering me along by saying, "*Wolf, Wolf, Wolf, Wolf!*" his voice somewhere between a bark and a declaration.

I wasn't the only target of his shenanigans. Shelby was also a subject of his relentless teasing. Hysterically, on one occasion, Grandpa developed an elaborate scheme to prank Shelby. My brother, who may not have even been a fresh teenager at the time, had built a lean-to against a tree several feet from my grandparents' front door. Grandpa warned him that a panther would take up the lean-to and make it his home, but Shelby quickly dismissed him.

While my brother was away, Grandpa rearranged some of the sticks that formed the lean-to and fabricated panther tracks around it. Later that evening when Shelby and a friend ventured out to the lean-to,a flashlight in hand, they quickly returned in a panic sure that a panther had invaded the hide-out. Grandpa played along and inspected the site claiming that indeed a panther had inhabited the lean-to. As luck would have it, Grandpa flashed his flashlight in the direction of the woods only to land the beam on a pair of glowing eyes from an unknown creature. Merely by chance, this affirmed his declaration to be true

"I warned you that a panther cat would take up roost here!" He hurried the boys back to the house. The whole time laughing so hard he could hardly keep a straight face.

It was Grandpa's intention to keep us aware of our environment and stay alert. I dare say we didn't go anywhere without first surveying our surroundings just in case we might see that old wolf or a panther cat. I can't help but think of the cruel irony now that it's him who is running to escape the wrath of a predator.

Now, his run was nearly over.

It made me smile knowing that everything Grandpa did with me had a purpose. His teasing, story-telling, inquisitive thoughts and propositions were all intended to teach something. While not always obvious at the time, I could see now the wisdom in every action.

Looking back, he crafted my sense-of-humor, developed my patience, made me attentive. He nurtured my sensitivities, emboldened me with confidence, and improved my intellect.

Grandpa instilled a toughness, built a strong work ethic within me, demonstrated morals and ethics, motivated me to persevere, taught me how to live, showed me how to love, and in the end, how to gracefully die.

As I looked in the rearview mirror, I realized Grandpa was part of my every fiber. My eyes mirrored the shape of his eyes. My brain was full of his thoughts, his ideas, his machinations. My heart harbored his way of loving, his way of expressing emotions, and his way of caring for others. Grandpa would live on through me and the others he influenced. This didn't come to fruition because he was intentional in making it that way. I am who I am because he was who he was. Because it was impossible for it to be any different.

I laughed at the realization and thought back to the wonderful memories of my time spent with him. My earliest, as a young boy riding on his lap while he drove a tractor. On his lap, I was on top of the world. He let me pretend to drive and enthusiastically gave me directions and told me when to turn the wheel. He constantly encouraged me, telling me what a good job I was doing.

Most evenings we sat together in his big chair after sharing a *Twinkie* and a cold glass of milk. His shoes off, legs extended to drape his feet over the footrest, with me squeezed in beside him – his arm around my shoulders hugging me close to his side. As I got older and couldn't fit beside him, I would stand behind the same chair and rub his head for quarters as he leaned back, relaxing at the end of a hard day. He was like *Tom,* the slinky black cat, in that way – always wanting some attention. At times, my brother and I rubbed that old man's head and back until our fingers cramped. Sometimes we did it out of love and others because we were motivated to do so.

One of Grandpa's favorite stories involved my brother and I rubbing his back. On a trip to the lake, we had caught a glimpse of a road sign that piqued our curiosity. The hand-painted sign suggested a canyon just off the highway. It seemed so mysterious, and our imaginations could hardly be contained. We pestered Grandpa for weeks about showing us the canyon. One day he finally relented and posed a proposition. If we would rub his back, our chances to see the canyon would increase by percentage points. If we reached 100%, then we could be certain to go.

We quickly agreed and massaged his back until we could hardly feel our hands. By the time we had reached the 80% mark, we pushed forward to the finish. We couldn't take the chance of not reaching 100% and seeing the mysterious canyon. As we edged closer to our goal, our progress moved slower and slower, our pace advancing in smaller increments.

"Ohhh, I think maybe we're at 82%." He lay flat on his stomach, arms limp, head turned comfortably to one side. His eyes shut, he spoke in tones that seemed to suggest it was an agonizing development to admit our chances were increasing. He milked it for all it was worth.

When we got to 99%, Grandpa continued to push our buttons by resorting to decimals.

"Maybe we're at 99.1% now…It could be 99.2%, but I'm just not sure."

"GRANDPA!" United in our frustration, we expressed the unfairness of it all. And in typical fashion, he laughed and continued to prod.

"Oh, I'd sure hate to get this close and still not be 100% sure of going to that canyon. It'd be a shame to leave it to chance."

When we objected to his ploy, he laughed harder.

After more than an hour we had finally reached 100%. Feeling entitled, we demanded that we go at once. To which he laughed and teased us about other things in ways to get more back rubbing. Then Grandma interjected.

"Norman Earl! Now get up! We're taking those boys to see that canyon."

"Okay, Momma." He sheepishly agreed while still laughing under his breath.

Upon this development, Shelby and I snickered feeling the satisfaction of victory.

Later that day when we arrived at the canyon, it was Grandpa who got the last laugh. Honestly, he always did.

The *canyon* we were so desperate to see was nothing more than a clever name for the housing community located off the highway. As we drove through, Shelby and I took it all in, disgusted. Grandpa bellowed with laughter as he slowly drove by each house.

"Isn't it wonderful?" He teased and carried on with laughter.

Grandma couldn't help but cover her mouth to hide how his shenanigans were tickling her.

"Just take us home," I said with resignation.

Shelby, quickly added in a flat tone, "I wished I'd have never even looked and just closed my eyes."

Grandpa loved to repeat Shelby's line for years afterward.

The driveway, the porch, the house with its warm glow. There were thousands of memories, stories, and lessons to relive. I wanted to playback all of them before pulling onto the highway. It seemed fitting that I would do it here as I saw so much more than a scene reflected in the mirror.

This time, "See you soon," didn't seem to fit.

For this, I was 100% certain.

CHAPTER TWENTY-ONE

Every Little Bit

Psalm 23:4 *"Even though I walk through the valley of the shadow of death, I will fear no evil, for you are with me; your rod and your staff, they comfort me."*

"I SAID GOODBYE."

I called Julia to tell her as soon as I could find the words after leaving my grandparents' drive.

"I'm so sorry, baby. Is there anything I can do for you?" Her words tinged with tears.

"No, sweetheart." I took a deep breath. "It is what it is."

I must have sounded defeated.

"You've got such a long drive ahead of you. I'm worried that maybe you're not okay to drive," she expressed a legitimate concern.

"I'll be okay. The drive will be good. It'll give me time to clear my head and process all of this."

"I'll be praying," she offered.

I bit down on my bottom lip to prevent a tearful outburst. "Okay, babe."

We said goodbye, and I continued to drive down the highway with my burdened heart and lonesome thoughts as silent passengers.

My subconscious mind somehow kept the truck between the never-ending lines as the rest of my being drifted away to a place of vague awareness. It was much like the place where the mind goes while reading from a book, word for word, only to get to the end of a page and realize you're unsure how you got to that point with no memory of a page full of words in front of you. This was me. Behind the wheel of my truck. Speeding down the highway.

A good distance had passed before the bright lights of oncoming traffic snapped me from the trance. I sat straight in my seat and adjusted the temperature. My clothes were damp from perspiration and sweat dripped from my brow. I needed to get my mind straight or find a distraction. So, I pressed an icon on my phone and dialed my mother.

"Hey, *Troll.*" It was her standard greeting for me. In fact, embarrassingly, I typically used it on her as well. But not this time.

"Hey, Mom."

She could tell right away, and her tone turned serious. "You okay?"

"I don't know."

"Grandpa?" She asked but already knew.

"I said goodbye."

"Do you want to talk about it?"

"I don't know." I truly didn't.

My mom sometimes took on deep philosophical views. Sometimes they seemed not to match the situation, but on this account, she knew just what to say. Her plain and simple response was what I needed.

"You know… Grandpa has lived a good life. You have done such a good job of supporting him and being with him through this whole time he's been sick. There's nothing else you can do. You got to say goodbye, right?"

"Yeah."

My single word response clouded with anxiety.

She reasoned, "That's more than most people ever get to do. When I lost my Daddy when I was pregnant with you, it didn't work out that way. I would have given anything to have had that chance."

"Yeah"

"I believe when it's our time to go, it's our time to go. God calls us home when he wants us home and there's not anything you or anybody else can do about that."

"…Okay." I didn't have the energy or the desire to argue.

"You don't have to believe me, but sometimes your mom can be right."

"Okay."

"You don't seem to agree with me – that's alright. You can think about it however you want. The point is... Grandpa couldn't have lived a better life, and you couldn't have asked for a better opportunity than you got to say goodbye."

She couldn't have been more right about the last point.

"True, but it doesn't make it any easier."

"I know, son, but he's lived 84 years. Lots of people don't get their grandparents for that long."

"All those years just gave me more time to love him. In some ways that makes it even harder," I quickly explained.

"You've got a point," she slowly agreed.

My response rendered my mom temporarily speechless something I thought was impossible.

"I should probably go," I stated.

"You sure you're okay? You don't sound like you're in a good place." Her concern was evident.

Unexpectedly, her statement prompted me to laugh.

It caught her off guard, and she laughed in response. "What's so funny?"

"Grandpa," I chuckled.

"What about him?"

"Mom, did you ever hear about the man that broke his arm in three places?"

"Huh?"

I tried to hold back my laughter to deliver the punchline.

"Yeah, I did him a big favor, told him to stay out of those places."

We both laughed and suddenly my eyes were wet with tears again, but they were happy tears from an unforgettable memory from a beautifully uncommon man.

My mom commented, "Well, I guess that helps."

I responded, "Just like the old woman standing in the ocean."

She laughed without understanding and encouraged me to explain.

I started without hesitation.

"One day a passerby saw an old woman standing knee-deep in the ocean. The passerby called out to the old woman and asked her what she was doing. She told him she was raising the water level of the ocean. He thought she was crazy and asked her just how she supposed she was doing that. She replied to him that she was peeing. The passerby shook his head and asked the woman just why she thought doing that was going to work. The old woman smiled and told the passerby, 'Well, that's easy - every little bit helps!'"

Mom loved it and reacted with laughter before offering an observation. "Grandpa was always trying to teach one thing or another, and I'm sure he'd be happy to know you remember so much."

"I think it's already being proven that everything I see, say or do, makes me think about him in some way."

"And that's something nobody can ever take away from you," she proclaimed.

"It's something I'll cherish."

I thanked her for the company, told her I loved her, hung up and retraced the last few days in my mind. It had all happened so fast as I looked back on it. Too fast. Not enough time. But any amount of time would never be enough.

My mind shifted directions, and I began thinking, considering the rest of my week. I was scheduled to be in a different city for the next four days. My work would end in Dallas on Thursday.

As my mind wandered, I couldn't help but wonder when he might pass on. Immediately, I felt guilty for leaving him. The mental torment he must be facing with death knocking at his door terrified me. I hurt for Grandma, Beverly, and Dad, everyone who had to witness his pain. Then, I considered the other loved ones, like Shelby, who wanted to be there but were unable. It was a swirling stew of emotions for what had been, what would be, and what I wished could be different. My own thoughts left me dizzy.

I pressed a button and lowered my window for fresh air. The pleasant rush against my face revived me temporarily, unburdening my sorrow.

With wonder, I peered to the sky and gazed upon countless stars twinkling brightly against an inky black sky. Their secrets seemed to flash a celestial code communicating with the heavens.

All I could think was, "There's no room for death on a night painted with such perfection."

With my eyes fixed above, the crisp night air blowing against my face, I closed my eyes and did something I thought I had forgotten how to do.

I muttered a simple prayer.

"Please, Dear God, be with us."

CHAPTER TWENTY-TWO

In Lieu Of Courage

JOSHUA 1:9 *"Have I not commanded you? Be strong and courageous. Do not be frightened, and do not be dismayed, for the Lord your God is with you wherever you go."*

"HE'S STILL WITH US."

My heart thumped against my chest as I read the text. Aunt Beverly had frequently updated me with messages since I had left my grandparents' home.

I hurried to the parking lot and jumped in my truck, started it up, and ignored the stop sign while pulling onto the street. My only concern was making the six-hour trip in five hours or less. I drove in ways that suggested other motorists should voluntarily yield the road to me. My best friend was holding on, refusing to surrender and I wasn't about to let speed limits, stop lights, or other motorists keep me from being by his side.

Glancing from my phone to the road, I pushed a button and called Beverly. Her voice came through the speakers of my truck.

"Hey," I spoke first as soon as I heard the connection.

"Hey," she said. Her voice was sad and heavy.

"How's he doing?"

"…Well…," her voice grew heavier, weighted with grief, "he's still with us, but I don't know for how much longer."

I stayed silent and pushed the accelerator to the floor.

She continued, "You know he's not had any food or water for several days. He's not opened his eyes all day… He's gasping for air with every breath."

I was pushing the truck to its limits. Pushing well beyond the limits of the law.

"Okay, I'm coming as fast as I can."

"Be careful."

"I will."

"Okay, love you. See you soon."

I hung up and frantically reexamined my route on the GPS. I was on the quickest path and blazing a trail behind me. I still had hours ahead of me, but I continued to drive as if I had minutes to get there.

For the next few hours, I sent Beverly text messages to update her on my progress, and she conveyed proof that my hazardous efforts to get there were justified. *He's still with us.* God only knows how. God only knew why.

My imagination ran blindly. Could Grandpa be hanging on just for me? The thought of it made me sick. I suddenly realized that he may have endured additional suffering for days simply because I had selfishly stated I would be back to see him. Even though I had told him it was okay to go, I had also implied it wasn't. The bile reached my throat as I admitted it was probably true.

"See you soon."

The truck jolted my body when I careened off the highway with four hot tires desperately grabbing for traction against the white rock. The house on the hill, veiled in the darkness of night, sat somberly in front of me while the drums thumped from my temples. With a deep breath, I drove carefully up the drive – all the while trying to suppress the volcanic pit of emotions that suddenly replaced the adrenaline that had been pumping tirelessly through my body for the past five hours. When I parked the truck, my head fell against the steering wheel. Exhausted and afraid, I squeezed my eyes shut and searched for the courage to open the truck door. I had driven nearly 400 miles like a maniac but, I struggled to force myself through the last 40 feet of the race. My search for courage futile, lost under these circumstances. Courage was for others.

All I had to do was what Grandpa had always asked from me.

With the words tumbling out like a fresh idea, I lifted my head from the steering wheel charged with a directive and put my thought into action.

"This ain't no step for a Stepper."

CHAPTER TWENTY-THREE

NOW

JOHN 3:16 *"For God so loved the world, that he gave his only Son, that whoever believes in him should not perish but have eternal life."*

THERE WOULD BE NO WORDS SPOKEN.

Silence commanded the room. Its occupants either unwilling or unable to speak.

Beverly greeted me first with a tear-choked hug. Her expression cradling swollen eyes and a mouth whose corners had fallen.

Grandma was a mirror-image of Beverly. She hugged me next and seemed reluctant to let go.

They had endured a front row seat to the extra-inning horror show. An agonizingly slow, deliberate and methodic takedown of a man they dearly loved who was finally succumbing to the inevitable. Since the day he was diagnosed, we had all known what the end result would be, but none of us could rightfully be prepared for what that looked like.

I focused my attention from the grieving women immediately in my life, to the man who had forecasted this moment. *"See you soon."*

With great trepidation, I took the remaining steps separating me from him.

In the four days, I had been absent, his appearance had changed. He looked completely emaciated, pale skin thin and brittle as it stretched around his skeletal frame. He showed no movement, flat upon his back, but for the survivalist mechanism that heaved his chest upward in desperate attempts to capture bits of oxygen. The movement and sound reminded me of a failing pump overcome with water.

As his chest lifted with grueling effort, each attempt produced a sickening sound. I didn't voluntarily kneel beside him; the sights and sounds forced me to my knees beside his bed.

The floor felt cold and hard and I instantly recognized it, but the gravity of the situation had rendered me helpless. I found it difficult to move as if I were trapped in a pool of gelatin which I desperately fought to escape.

When I reached for his hand, I found it to be still, limp and without circulation. I caressed it with both of my hands, wishing to rub it back to life. But there was no response. The last of his remaining energy had retreated to his core to pump slivers of air in and out of his failing body.

His face absent of expression, rested in a position turned in my direction. Life had abandoned his eyes leaving them sealed like a condemned building. While I held little hope, I wondered if somehow, he would recognize my voice.

"Grandpa, I'm here." The words crawled out from where they hid.

There was no visible sign that he had heard me.

I burst into tears. Emotion came in tsunami-like waves. My body shook as I sank lower against his bedside. An inaudible reaction to the pain, I called his name and said words that expressed objection to what was happening to him. Mumbled strings of words escaped without thought or reservation. Repeatedly I told him I loved him and apologized for it ending this way.

Through weeping eyes soaked with unbridled emotion, I noticed the whites of his eyes peeking under half-hooded lids. A single tear had trickled from the corner of his eye, staining part of his cheek. His pupils darted back and forth with urgency. I interpreted the deliberate movements as a desperate effort to communicate. But sadly, I was no more able to decipher his attempt than that of the stars in the night sky.

In response to him, I manufactured a smile and simply nodded in a knowing way.

"Grandpa, I love you." No other words would more appropriately fill the space.

At this, his pupils flashed, and another tear formed in the corner of his eye.

I felt helpless to understand his message. It clearly harbored importance, and it left me to only imagine what he wanted or needed me to know.

His eyes grew heavier and his pupils slowed. I recognized our window was closing. I sought to share how much he meant to me before it was too late.

"Thank you…Thank you for everything you've ever done for me…" I gulped in reaction to the words coming from my mouth, before finishing my thought, "…Thank you for being my Grandpa.

His eyelids closed like stage curtains. The final act. The show was over.

I hid my head between outstretched arms. An emptiness exploded in my heart and infiltrated every cell in my body. A cold numbness replaced the warm emotions of sorrow. The moment had turned to a scene being lived by another character. An experience so painful that reality had disappeared leaving only remnants of the physical and emotional torment that had seeded itself in the depths of my soul. I held this position silently on a schedule of my own.

Once composed, I released his hand, leaned over his body and rested my cheek against his. My fallen tears moistened the surface between his leathery skin and the youthful feel of mine. I fought the urge to hold onto him forever. Never letting him go. Never giving up. Never.

Instead, I braved a whisper in his ear. This time I spoke without conditions.

"It's okay, Grandpa – You can go, now."

CHAPTER TWENTY-FOUR

TESTED

Hebrews 11:6 *"And without faith it is impossible to please him, for whoever would draw near to God must believe that he exists and that he rewards those who seek him."*

"GRANDPA PASSED." Her words plain and matter-of-fact, her gentle touch waking me from an exhausted sleep.

After leaving his side, I had hugged Grandma, and stumbled down the hallway to my grandfather's room and collapsed on the bed. Now, looking at my phone resting on the table next to me, I realized I must have drifted off for close to an hour.

When I left, Beverly had moved a chair next to Grandpa's bed, held his hand for what would be his final breaths.

After she had delivered the sobering news, my aunt swiftly left my room to take care of the difficult tasks that follow any death. I swiveled from the bed and rubbed at my eyes before stumbling the length of the hallway once more, in the opposite direction and for another reason.

The front room where Grandpa had left this earth was made dark but for a single lamp casting a yellowish glow against the wall in the corner. Its presence created shadows over Grandpa's lifeless body, settled peacefully beneath the wall of windows in the room. Other than a large-faced clock counting seconds with incessant mechanical ticks, nothing detracted me from hearing the seesawing of my own breath.

Beverly had stepped outside making all the calls that are necessary when someone passes. Grandma mourned alone in the kitchen. As for me, I stood rooted to the floor at least twenty feet away, staring at Grandpa's body from across the room.

I had never been so near death, and the undesirable experience left me confused with my feelings. Part of me wanted to move to the body, hold his hand, kiss his forehead, breathe in one last whiff of his hair, but another part of me, a bigger part of me, resisted. A virtual tug-of-war took shape in my mind, with the *Don't Do It* team winning the moment.

I reasoned that he was gone and what remained wasn't any more part of him than the shell is to an egg. What I loved so much about him was now beyond my reach – the yoke was missing. So, I stood, my tears exhausted, lost without direction.

When Beverly walked back into the house, she detailed the calls she had been made. I was immediately impressed with her strength in the situation. Very procedural-like she counted off who had been contacted and recited what needed to yet be done. Her hand found the middle of my back as she spoke, and she rubbed circles on it while I stood, unresponsively.

She looked in the kitchen to Grandma and told her that a hospice nurse was on the way.

The nurse walked through the same door as I had walked through some three hours earlier. Her arrival seemed to bring a sense of calm and for me personally, relief. The sound of her voice had an authentic sound to it as she offered comforting words.

After asking for permission, she immediately cared for Grandpa's vacant body by washing and dressing him. The nurse expressed her kindness with a soft voice and demonstrated a gentle touch as she expertly maneuvered from one part of the corpse to the next. She spoke in apologetic tones while rearranging his arms and legs and then looked to us with sad eyes that expressed genuine empathy.

By the time the sweet nurse had finished tending to Grandpa's remains, the sheriff arrived to pronounce the death to be official. I watched all of this unfold from a safe distance, as if outside my own body. None of it seemed to be part of a reality I could understand. I had thought of this moment and had even predicted exactly how I might act, but quickly I learned that having a nightmare and living a nightmare were two very different monsters.

The sheriff said several kind words to all of us and then reached his hand outward in my direction. I greeted his gesture with a cold handshake. We held each other's stare for a moment. He then spoke directly to me, but his words fell on deaf ears. In response, I simply nodded my head in a show of appreciation. However, in some bizarre way, the handshake seemed to shake me from my trance. The passive being of numbness started to fade, replaced by an acute awareness of what had been lost forever.

Dull sadness stood on the corner, as my blood suddenly ran hot. My knuckles grew sharp while I surveyed the room in search of a fine place to stick my fist through the wall. Every muscle in my face grew tense. My teeth ground together as my breathing intensified. I shook my head with disgust, and an intense anger could be seen in the transformation of my posture. No longer despondent, I was now ready to lash out. Afraid of finding the wrong target, I removed myself from the room and stormed out of the house stomping onto the front porch.

I plopped into my chair and looked at his. Empty. Never to be occupied by his wonderful soul again. No more front porch chats; no more life lessons. Where laughter once flourished, only silence remained. The type of eternal silence that boasts victory by the symbolism of a vacant chair once occupied by a man who made everything better by merely being there.

I looked away from the chair and my heartache shifted into tears of rage.

"NO", my shout so loud it echoed and returned to me like a boomerang.

I angrily yelled into the darkness.

"WHY?"

But I knew why – Cancer.

Screw you Cancer!

I made known my displeasure for the repulsive, disgusting, loathsome disease that had stolen from me. I cursed it. I shouted it down. Yelling vulgarities, I jumped to my feet as If I had found my target but slowly relented when its cowardly face could not be found.

My eyes reddened from crying, my hair disheveled from the gripping of an unstable head. The rabidity grew from within.

Posed for a fight, I turned and looked at the sky. A wry smile was born upon my face, and I held a strong finger pointed to the sky. I had to put a face to my anger.

My attention turned to God.

"GOD!" I roared.

"YOU DID THIS!"

It was satisfying to finally face Him. Immediately, I stopped running, something I had been doing my entire life. Full stop, this was it, I turned toward God, seeking to confront Him and lay the blame of my pain at His feet.

"HOW could you DO THIS!"

My voice began to break, but the volume did not.

"YOU!"

"YOU LET HIM SUFFER!"

I bawled.

"…HOW DARE YOU, GOD!"

I stood firmly waiting for a response. Any response. A bolt of lightning, the opening of the skies, anything. Instead only the darkness and the orchestra of muted sounds accompanying it.

I dropped a shaking finger held to the sky and desperately searched for the calm in this storm of emotion and grief.

When I found it, my face transformed with a look of sudden realization – an epiphany.

Mocking laughter replaced my anger.

It wasn't God. God had no part in this. The realization was clear to me in that moment. My head moved back and forth tempting a sinister laugh.

"It couldn't be you… …YOU. DON'T. EXIST!"

My voice stronger, I stated it as a certain fact, and there wasn't an atheist alive who could have spoken it with more conviction or clarity.

With nothing left to say, I walked back to the door, pausing before entering. A fleeting thought stopped me from moving forward. *What would Grandpa think of my outburst?*

Suddenly ashamed, I felt an enormous guilt creeping into my mind. But, regardless, I stubbornly decided to stand by my actions but for one condition.

Twisting back to the darkness, spoken with a voice barely heard, I offered a proposition.

"If you do exist, prove it… Prove to me that you're there… Show me I'm wrong."

With that, I turned to the door, pushed it inward, and slammed it shut behind me.

CHAPTER TWENTY-FIVE

RECEIVED

MALACHI 3-10 *"'Bring the whole tithe into the storehouse, that there may be food in my house. Test me in this,' says the Lord Almighty, 'and see if I will not throw open the floodgates of heaven and pour out so much blessing that there will not be room enough to store it.'"*

CLICKETY-CLACK-CLICKETY-CLACK...

The rapid tapping of the keys clamored in the background as the sweet hospice nurse worked alone on her laptop from the kitchen table.

Meanwhile, Grandma, Beverly, and I sat together, and yet in complete solitude, in separate chairs positioned near one another in the living room.

The emptiness of the room, the presence of emotions spent, the absence of shared words, it all seemed to characterize the moment.

I sat lonesome in a chair, attempting to calm the inner-storm of guilt, regret, grief, and other tangled feelings I could not explain. My fight with God had left me unsettled and weakened. I didn't want to think any more about it, or anything else. So, I stared blankly into a realm of nothingness – transitioning back to feeling comfortably numb.

Cancer had prematurely stolen Grandpa from my life. Not like a sneaky thief who operates in the dark of night, but rather unabashedly announcing its presence with cold audacity. While born in his lung, it never attempted to hide, the mass was easily detectable by X-ray, and once observed, it seemed to dare Grandpa to treat it. Doing so would likely require surgery, bouts of chemotherapy and rounds of nausea-inducing cocktails leaving anyone of my grandpa's age to reconsider. For a man who believed in living his life, treating the disease was never a real consideration.

Once the perpetrator began to advance, it couldn't have anticipated the strength and resolve of its victim. Grandpa was hardened and tested in the cotton fields during the Great Depression, pushed to the limit while in the Navy, serving during the Korean War. He worked in factories, built businesses, and hustled cattle like the cowboy he was born to be. Surrounded by loved ones, fueled by an unyielding tenacity, and fortified by faith, Grandpa refused to give in, and never once gave cancer the satisfaction of hearing him complain.

In dealing with the intruder, he first chose to ignore it, never admitting it was there. When they told him that he had merely months to survive, he laughed at the prognosis and proved cancer wrong by pressing on, outliving their predictions. Then, when it dizzied him, he defied it by keeping his feet. Finally, when cancer took away his breath, he once again got the last laugh by gracefully exiting on his own terms.

Cancer may have eventually gotten him, but it didn't come out unscathed. Grandpa fought to the end.

When I looked across to Grandma, I couldn't help but feel a deep pain in my heart. Over 60-years of marriage to a man who filled her cup to the brim. He knew all the endings to her every sentence and fathered the son and daughter she held so dear. The patriarch was more than a branch on the family tree, he was the root that anchored it.

I glanced at Beverly. She held her head low resting on a balled-up hand. *Daddy's little girl.* The two of them had shared so many precious moments together. She adored him in every way, and probably had done so before she knew how to dress herself or tie her shoes. And as much as she cherished him, he loved her back in spades.

It was a terribly sad scene.

We were all startled when the sound of music tunneled through the hallway, filling the front room with the angelic sound of a harp. The three of us looked to one another with honest confusion, each questioning the next with speechless expressions.

I eased from my chair and followed the sound to the bedroom where I had fallen asleep after saying my final goodbye. On the nightstand, my phone was shining bright and emanating a song highlighted by the strumming of a harp. It was a tune I had never heard before and I was perplexed as to why my phone had come to life.

I picked up my phone from the nightstand, pushed a button to mute the blaring sound, unplugged it and curiously examined it while walking down the hall.

When I arrived at the edge of the front room, I announced to the group, "The music was coming from my phone and I have no idea why."

Without hesitation, the sweet nurse directed a question to me, "What time is it?"

I looked at my phone and answered, "It's 4:44."

She asked another question, but this time with a smile, "You know what that means?"

I didn't and indicated so with my head.

Her voice changed from soft to convincing, retaining its kinder tones as she explained. "444 represents the angels. They are here to comfort you – to let you know that everything is okay. God is talking to you."

I stood with a disbelieving expression that could have been taken for annoyance. I meant no disrespect to the sweet nurse, but it didn't make sense to me. By the time I took my seat in the living room,

Beverly had already researched it on her phone and was leaning toward me to show the proof.

"Look, it's wonderful. The angels are letting us know that Dad's okay." She seemed genuinely relieved by the revelation.

Respectfully, I gave it a look and faked a smile in response.

I wasn't convinced. I turned to my phone and tried to determine why it had malfunctioned. When I looked at my alarm setting, an alarm had been programmed for 4:44 am. But that couldn't have been possible, I had woken the previous morning at 6:00 a.m. and had no need or reason for another alarm. And no way would I have ever set one at such an early or random time. It left me perplexed.

While we all continued to sit in our places, I turned my phone off, leaned my head back and closed my eyes. For the next hour or so, I drowned myself with skepticism, excusing away all that had occurred. *There had to have been a glitch in my iPhone.*

But...

How could I explain the sound of harps that played a song I had never heard?

Why was an alarm set at 4:44 a.m.?

What were the chances that the sweet nurse who was sent to our home, not only knew about the meaning of 444 but also was present to tell me?

As the sun began to peek over the horizon, I walked down the drive with my phone in hand. Julia had been waiting anxiously, hours away, with our kids, back in Nebraska. She had not heard from me since I had texted her to let her know I had safely arrived from Dallas.

When she answered my call, she knew by the sound of my greeting.

"I'm so sorry sweetheart," her words were consoling. Her voice served as the virtual hug I craved from the love of my life.

Generically, I described how my last moments with him had unfolded. It was brief and I left out most of the horrific details. It was too soon, and impossible to completely admit how his death had devastated me and led me to curse at God and deny his very existence.

I nearly ended the connection, before deciding to share one point.

"Before I let you go, I have to tell you, the strangest thing happened at 4:44 this morning."

She interrupted, "Wait, I don't know what you're going to say, but before you do, I have to tell you what happened here."

I found her interruption odd but agreed to let her go first.

"At exactly 4:44 this morning, Jackson woke me as I heard him from his room through the baby monitor sitting on the dresser. I know that it was 4:44 because my alarm clock was sitting next to the monitor." She swallowed and took in a deep breath before continuing. "When I walked over to his room, I found him sitting up on his bed."

"Was he crying?" I interjected.

"No, that's just it – he wasn't. Which is not like him if he wakes in the night. Instead, he was happy and just babbling about something. When I first heard it, I couldn't understand what he was doing, but then as I listened, I figured it out."

"What was it?" She had my full attention.

"Toys. Jerrad, he was talking about his toys – on and on – he kept talking about his toys."

My body tingled when I heard her explain.

In an avalanche of revelation, my doubting brain started connecting the dots.

My phone.

The alarm.

The harp-like song.

The sweet nurse there to explain it all.

Jackson awakened.

Not being upset.

Talking about his toys as he often did with Grandpa.

And all of this…After my challenge issued to God…

"Are you still there?" Julia knew but poked me to break the silence.

"Yeah," but I wasn't.

"So… what were you going to tell me about 4:44?"

CHAPTER TWENTY-SIX

ASKED

JEREMIAH 33-3 *"Call to me and I will answer you, and will tell you great and hidden things that you have not known."*

"GRANDPA'S PROBABLY SITTING ON A POND BANK RIGHT ABOUT NOW."

Shelby said it as I rode with him to the cemetery following the service at the church. I peered through my passenger window and thought back to the day Grandpa and I had spent visiting the creek, his childhood home, and his final resting place.

It still seemed surreal that he was gone, and I liked Shelby's idea. The thought of Grandpa doing what he loved doing most made me smile. Someday, I hoped to be reunited and sit beside him, bask in the heavenly sun, and once again, share laughter with my best friend.

As we arrived, the cemetery grounds, as well as the weather, were reminiscent of my previous visit. I, among others, carried the casket to the designated area marked by a temporary canopy set above an open gash in the ground where Grandpa's remains would be lowered, buried, and left to rest.

I looked around, before taking a seat, only to see various forms of weeping eyes cemented upon familiar faces. Beverly and my dad sat on either side of Grandma, sandwiching her with love. Beverly's daughter, Misty, stood with her head tilted to one side and embraced me before I sat. Her blonde hair shimmered in a way that matched the tears in her eyes. As she held me, I couldn't help but think about how Grandpa loved to tease her about Peter Cottontail.

As a little girl, Misty was always welcomed by Grandpa with a song.

"Here comes Peter Cottontail…"

"Hopping down the bunny trail…"

To finish, he reached to the bottom of his lungs to find a deeper, louder sound.

"HIPPETY - HIPPETY HOPPING ALONG!"

Grandpa loved to tell the story as to how the little girl suddenly changed course. After years of hearing the song and smiling along, one random day, Misty, having waited for Grandpa to finish, replied to him by saying, "I just hate that song."

Now, while enjoying her hug, I heard Grandpa's voice singing the words in perfect tune.

The graveside service was equally as beautiful as the church service had been. The Navy had sent a trio of cadets who played Taps from brass trumpets. The preacher delivered poignant words. Family and friends shared condolences with sad smiles and open arms.

Beverly kissed me on the cheek and smiled at me in a way that confessed everything. She and I had always been close but now the two of us shared something that only we could fully understand. I squeezed her in a way to let her know that I knew.

Grandma showed more strength than I could have ever expected, and I already held a high opinion for her resolve. When I wrapped my arms around her, she told me she loved me and whispered to me how proud Grandpa would have been of me for the eulogy I had tearfully delivered at the church. I loved her back and wanted her to know that she was every bit as important to me as Grandpa had been.

Finally, I hugged my dad. I did so with forgiveness as Grandpa had encouraged me to do back when we sat by the creek. Nothing my dad had ever done was anything worth harboring a grudge. And, as he had correctly told me about the decisions he made when I was a kid, "Someday, I would understand." As I looked at him, I could see the pride he had for me, while also seeing the deep sadness he held over losing his father. Now, I recognized that my dad was the most direct link I had to my grandpa, and that was something worth appreciating.

As others were headed to their cars, I approached the preacher who lingered by the graveside. I extended my hand to thank him for how he had honored my grandpa with a perfect service.

"Thank you, sir — thank you for everything."

"You're welcome, son."

There was another reason I had sought to speak with him. In the days prior to the funeral, he had learned of the experience I had encountered with 444, as well as the events that precipitated it.

"Can I ask you a question?"

He nodded and showed me his full attention.

"There's just one thing I can't get past."

"And what's that, son?"

The answer seemed to squeeze through the tight expression from my face.

"Of all of us, why me? Why did God choose to communicate with me? Why not Beverly? She loved Grandpa as much as I did. Why not Grandma? She had been in his life longer than any of us. Why not my dad, Shelby, Misty? Why me?" I was truly exasperated.

The preacher smiled and looked at me with wise eyes as if I might be the only one who didn't know. He extended a hand, placed it on my shoulder and explained it in the simplest terms.

"Well, you asked him, didn't ya?"

CHAPTER TWENTY-SEVEN

Melvin

PROVERBS 17-22 "'A joyful heart is good medicine, but a crushed spirit dries up the bones."

"WHEEEEEEEEEEEEEEEEEERE'S GRANDMA?"

She giggled with the way I greeted her on the call, and I imagined her doing so with the tip of her tongue peeking between her teeth.

Where's Grandma being a game Grandpa liked to play. Any time I rushed into my grandparents' house as a young boy, finding Grandpa alone, he would greet me by echoing my question with a bellow and deep laugh.

"Well let's see..."

He may have won an Oscar for acting as if he didn't know. Rubbing his chin with his eyes searching for a long lost-thought, served only to increase my aggravation.

"GRANDPA!" I impatiently protested.

"Well, she might be in Tallahassee... but I really don't know." My agitation brought fuel to his laughter. "Then again, she could be in Kalamazoo."

This giving me reason to stomp my feet and shake my head. "GRANDPA!"

"Oh, Oh…," a sudden realization, "I know where she is…"

And even though I was sure of what he was likely to say, my thirst for wanting to know where she might be, kept me attentive to his words.

He held out a giant finger upward and gestured with it as to punctuate his action with an exclamation point. "She's in the Grandma Locker under *G*!"

It rankled me every time. Often leaving him to swiftly reach out to grab my arm to prevent me from running away in protest. When his laughter dissipated, he usually arrived at the truth.

Now, on the phone, Grandma played along.

"Well, let's see…" she said.

And, with her response, we shared a laugh.

"How are you, Angel?"

"Pretty tolerable-like, thank you." This, another of Grandpa's favorites.

She giggled, again.

"You know, nobody will ever have to miss Grandpa with you around."

I smiled from my end.

"Grandma, I miss him."

"Me, too. Every single day."

Immediately I hurt for her.

"It's been more than a year but still feels like yesterday," I said.

"You know, I feel him with me all the time. Sometimes I can just imagine him standing behind me or telling me what to do and what not to do. When I'm watching a show on TV, I'll laugh and find myself looking over to his chair to see if he's laughing with me. I have to stop myself when I hear that I've started talking to him and then I realize he's not there."

Hearing this, I started to choke up. A lighter moment was needed.

"Grandma, do you remember when Grandpa was starting to feel pretty sick? When he only had maybe three months or so to live? And even though he felt that way, he kept on making people laugh. The time I'm thinking about the most is when Davey was visiting."

She laughed right away, as she knew the story well.

"Melvin," she blurted it out between bursts of laughter.

Grandpa was certainly not feeling well and spent most days in his chair, feet out with a blanket covering his legs. He was aided by oxygen and slept upright for most of the day. One particular day, my cousin from my mother's side, who also happened to be my childhood best-friend, stopped by to check on Grandpa. When Davey pulled up the driveway, Grandpa decided to lay limp where he sat in his chair. He then lifted the covers to his chin and closed his eyes.

Davey walked into the room moving slowly and tears formed at the edges of his eyes. He loved my Grandpa as everyone did. As he approached Grandpa's chair, he extended a gentle hand and placed it on Grandpa's shoulder. With that, Grandpa bellowed out an agonizing cry, followed by opening his eyes ever-so-slightly.

Davey stared down at him with great concern expressed with a sympathetic smile.

Grandpa called out to him pretending not to recognize him.

"Meeeeeeeeelvin?... Oh, Melvin… Is that you, Melvin?"

Davey's expression was priceless as his eyebrows lifted with worrying eyes. Instantly, he swiveled to me as if to say, '*Oh no, he's worse than I thought!*'

Grandpa shucked the covers from his chin and showed his silent laugh – that signature laugh. He reached up for a hug from Davey and laughed a little more.

Nothing more embodied his spirit or could do more to characterize him than his approach to his own mortality. Clearly, he never wanted anyone to feel sorry for him – he only wanted people to laugh.

Those who knew him best, will always remember him for the kind soul who loved to joke, loved to tease, and loved to bring joy into every situation, no matter the circumstances.

CHAPTER TWENTY-EIGHT

444

ISAIAH 43-10 *"'You are my witnesses," declares the Lord, "and my servant whom I have chosen, that you may know and believe me and understand that I am he."*

"JULIA, IT HAPPENED, AGAIN."

It had become a common refrain, as the number sequence continued to follow me in every aspect of my life. Indeed, I had demanded for God to prove Himself.

It was something, He never had to do, but He chose to do it. And He did so in ways I would never be able to cast off as happenstance or coincidence. In the beginning, I started waking at exactly 4:44, then the numbers started appearing to me on road signs, gas pumps, television programs, radio broadcasts, ballgames, billboards, phone numbers, dash readings, GPS estimates, bank statements, credit cards, restaurant receipts, and in a multitude of other ways.

More importantly, the numbers were shown to me in instances when I felt sadness while thinking about my grandpa, or at times when my faith had started to waver.

Despite all of God's efforts, I still allowed skepticism to impact my faith. When presented with the number sequence I sought to ignore it. They were numbers I no longer wanted to see. I felt haunted and stalked by what I evolved into viewing as nothing more than coincidences.

Over time, I began to document my experiences by taking pictures concerning the numerical happenings in my life. At last count, there had been more than 200 occurrences where 444 was shown to me. All this since Grandpa's passing, less than two years ago.

I finally began to accept it on a Friday afternoon just before Mother's Day. I had been stressed from work and took the afternoon to exercise and blow off steam. There was mounting pressure from my work, the challenges of consistently being a good husband and father were ever-present, I still mourned the loss of my grandpa – missing him every day, and 444 had started appearing more frequently, forcing me to think more about its meaning.

My head felt as if it might explode and I desperately wanted to get away from it all by working up a sweat and checking out from reality while pumping the pedals of the elliptical machine.

As I worked into a sticky lather, my efforts were going as planned. Blankly, I stared through a large window showing the view of an empty parking lot. My heart pumped with intensity while my mind found an easy place to rest.

The workout was proving therapeutic and I had nearly fallen into a dream-like state before being snapped back to a state of awareness. An indescribable bolt of thought shot through my brain. It possessed crystal-like clarity, immersed in deep purpose and fueled by a unique type of inspiration. The experience left my entire body tingling. Immediately, and unlike me to think so, my mind turned to God.

The God I had ignored, despite his answer.

The God I had run from my entire life.

The God who I repeatedly denied.

The God who forgave me.

The one heavenly father who despite my life of sin, kept pursuing my soul.

I let my thought escape from my mouth. *"Is God talking to me?"*

Then I dismissed it as soon as I had considered it.

In that moment of dismissal, I looked at the elliptical screen to check my progress.

The bright LED display flashed against my eyes.

Abruptly, I stopped pedaling and jumped from the machine.

4.44.

I had traveled 4.44 miles.

The revelation took the wind from my lungs. I backed against a wall, placed my hands on my knees while leaning forward. It was there that I attempted to find my breath while I pondered the thought that had exploded in my brain.

Could I really do what God had just asked me to do?

CHAPTER TWENTY-NINE

Unlikely

---

1 Corinthians 1: 27-29 "'But God chose the foolish things of the world to shame the wise; God chose the weak things of the world to shame the strong. God chose the lowly things of this world and the despised things—and the things that are not—to nullify the things that are, so that no one may boast before him."

"I FEEL LIKE I MUST BE THE MOST UNLIKELY PERSON FOR GOD TO CHOOSE."

Julia and I sat in matching rocking chairs on our front porch as I played back for her the way God seemingly spoke to me earlier in the day.

"I support you in whatever you do," she confirmed her sincerity by reaching for my hand.

I shook my head in disbelief.

"I'm so unqualified. Why would God choose me?"

"I don't know, sweetheart, but it's not for us to say who God chooses and who he doesn't."

Her faith had always been much stronger than mine.

She continued, "Maybe you should just start listening to what's happening in your life."

She was right, but after years of denying God, ignoring His efforts to communicate, and essentially, turning my back on him in every instance, it left me bewildered as to why He would continue pursuing my soul.

It was a level of forgiveness beyond my imagination, sunk in the depths of an unconditional love I could never give.

That night, after we put the kids in bed, our earlier conversation was reborn in the living room. Julia and I rehashed it and explored the idea from various angles. Unfortunately, it led me to no clearer conclusion than previously found. Seemingly the more we talked about it, the more confused I felt.

Frustrated I turned on the TV and flipped to a basketball game. When the game appeared on the screen, one team was at the free throw line. The clock was stopped with a certain amount of time left in the contest. I tossed the remote and looked to Julia. By the time she realized why I was staring at her, my feeling of incredulity turned to laughter.

"I give up." I threw my hands into the air and walked from the room as Julia continued to laugh.

Two days later, Julia asked if I would like to go to church. It was Mother's Day, and I knew she wanted to go. I was not a regular attendee, and it wasn't where I wanted to be, but this was her day, and because of that, I agreed.

We tucked the kids away in their respective areas after arriving at the church, where one would learn about Jesus, one would be appeased by bubbles, and the other would be held and rocked. Then, Julia and I found spots near the last row. Songs were sung, announcements made, and the sermon was ready to be delivered.

When the pastor walked to the front of the stage, Julia gave me a grudging nod for permission to browse on my phone during the sermon.

As the pastor began to speak, I found myself unexpectedly listening to her words.

She began with this, "Before I begin, I have to tell everyone something. Right before I took the stage, God spoke to me. He said that I was to deliver a message to someone sitting here in this service. This is my third service today, and I didn't say this in the others. God was explicit in telling me that someone in this crowd has been chosen. He has asked you to do something. He said you don't want to do this because you are someone who feels unlikely, unqualified."

Julia nudged me and looked at me with a serious set of eyes.

"She's talking about you!" It was intended to be a whisper but came out much louder.

I shook my head and motioned for her to hush so that we didn't bring unwanted attention.

The pastor went on speaking in ways that seemed to reflect the conversation Julia and I had shared on the front porch. By the time she finished, I had long-since set my phone aside, becoming fully attentive. Her final statement on the matter then echoed in my mind.

"Remember," she stated, "God doesn't choose the qualified, rather he qualifies the chosen."

After the service, I processed the total sum of it all. I spent the next month deliberately praying with sincere intent.

I asked for God to show me what He wanted from me. Then, after overwhelming and continual proof witnessed through my ongoing experiences, I finally agreed to accept what God had asked me to do.

Per his instruction, I would faithfully share how God made me a witness using 444 to prove his eternal glory.

Now at peace, thanks to the Ever-Lasting Grace and Undaunting Love from God, I run from Him no more.

EPILOGUE

Look

---

1 John 4:16 *"'And so we know and rely on the love God has for us. God is Love. Whoever lives in love lives in God, and God in them."*

My life serves as an example that God never gives up on any of us. Each one of us has a purpose, and God seeks to use us in ways to glorify His kingdom. His ways may not be obvious to us, and they may not be what we would choose for ourselves. But His are choices to be honored.

When God called me to serve His purpose, I was reluctant.

Before His calling, I would have scoffed at the idea that I, the most unlikely of options, would be selected to do God's work. So, when He clearly spoke to me, I couldn't understand why.

Ever since I took my first step away from God, He followed me in a relentless pursuit. I never game Him credit when He deserved it. Even when His presence was glaringly obvious, I chose to look away. But our God is merciful, forgiving, loving, and almighty.

God's use of 444 in my life change me from a staunch non-believer to those of a true believer. I'm ashamed to admit that I looked at God so blindly, and I'm embarrassed that I lived a life far removed from His.

But **our God forgives**. He pursues His children without restraint and will use you in His way, for His glory just as He uses me.

In the end, it was never about why He chose me, it was simply that He did.

Once I understood that key difference, I was able fully yield and open my heart to His ways.

When I reflected on my relationship with my grandpa, I noticed there were parallels between my relationship with him and the one I eventually sought with Christ. This starts with an uncompromising reciprocal love that is to be cherished, protected, and never forgotten. It goes on with a collection of characteristics Grandpa sought to instill in me.

What I had thought was nothing more than a collection of silly stories meant to make me laugh, were actually life lessons Grandpa had always known I needed. His clever storytelling taught me about faith, forgiveness, trust, introspection, love, and life itself. These are lessons I'll pass on to my children. Therefore, Grandpa's legacy will endure through the eyes of my kids: Hannah, Jackson, Cameron, and Penelope.

Because of Grandpa, I found Christ – for that, I owe him my eternity. Grandpa's actions were meant to lead me on that path throughout his life, but it wasn't until his death that I was reborn.

God redeemed my soul. He never stopped trying.

If you've been running…slow down…dare a glance over your shoulder…and you'll see…

He's pursuing you as well.

36000561R00114

Made in the USA
Lexington, KY
09 April 2019